DAY TO DAY
ANXIETY MANAGEMENT

Day to Day Anxiety Management

E. Lakin Phillips, Ph.D.

 ROBERT E. KRIEGER PUBLISHING COMPANY
HUNTINGTON, NEW YORK
1977

Original Edition 1977

Printed and Published by
ROBERT E. KRIEGER PUBLISHING CO., INC.
645 NEW YORK AVENUE
HUNTINGTON, NEW YORK 11743

Copyright © 1977 by
ROBERT E. KRIEGER PUBLISHING CO., INC.

Printed in the United States of America

Library of Congress Cataloging in Publication Data

Phillips, Ewing Lakin, 1915-
    Day to day anxiety management.

    1. Anxiety.   2. Self-actualization (Psychology)
I. Title.
BF575.A6P49   158'.1   76-26581
ISBN 0-88275-460-2

Contents

Preface to Readers

You will get more out of this book if you will read it and use it differently from the way you read most books.

Most major points and even some minor ones are followed by living examples—examples from the lives of people grappling with the same problems you and your friends have. Pay attention to these examples and try to select similar situations from your own life that parallel the written ones.

Think to yourself—and talk to yourself—about these points and examples, and try to realize how they can actually be made to apply to your own situation which you, of course, know better than anyone else in the world. Try to avoid generalities, stay with the specifics, when dealing with situations from your own life that match examples from the book.

Take time to learn what you've read—just knowing in the sense of passive reading, while a good start, will not do the job as well for you.

Although the tendency toward, or the capacity for, anxiety is innate in the human nervous system, the specific anxieties you harbor are learned and can therefore be unlearned (overcome), or brought under better control so that the anxiousness is not as disruptive or burdensome.

At the end of each chapter STOP and TELL yourself what you have read; say it aloud to yourself (or write down the essence of what you have learned or noted about yourself); and then move on to some applications to your own life.

Author's Preface

Today many popular books on self-help, self-development, personal
effectiveness and mental health appear to make great promise
to the reader. There is a kind of "make-a-new-man (or woman)-
out-of-yourself" theme running throughout many of these books
which claim to be yours—Mr. or Mrs. Reader—if you will but
partake of the great wisdom offered.

The theme in this book is different. While increases in personal
comfort and effectiveness through better self management may
sometimes show dramatic results, the emphasis in this book is
placed more modestly on *teaching you what you can do and how
you can go about helping yourself as you now live.* No glittering
promises of wholly new worlds are made.

You can, without trying to make yourself over in toto, avail yourself of more relaxed and enjoyable living by following some fairly
common and tested routines. You can learn how to *capitalize on
information you already have*; or you may possibly learn new
things about yourself which can serve your self-development and
self-actualization purposes. Although this book provides guidelines and many suggestions and illustrations in regard to handling
anxiety, the actual usage is up to you. The more you employ
the tactics and strategies suggested, the better are your chances
of anxiety reduction and self improvement.

Good luck and good reading!

Introduction

Someone said, "Anxiety is with us always."

Philosophers have remarked that we are ". . . living in an age of anxiety."

A poet said, "To be anxious is to be human."

Surely everyone experiences anxiety, more or less severe at times. You may remember your most anxious time, a time where you felt a paralyzing lump in your stomach, a dry and parched throat, and a feeling of wanting to run, shout, flail your arms, or even jump out of your skin—to get away from the tension.

This paralyzing time may have been when you were waiting to hear "yes" or "no" to an issue vital to your future, a decision rendered by others that was to have long-range consequences in your life. Such decisions are often made by others with little or no direct inputs from yourself. You felt helpless and anxious.

Once the decisive time is over, whether the outcome is good or bad for the anxiety-ridden person, tensions do subside, and one feels somewhat better. This issue is settled for the moment. BUT we are subject to the same tensions again . . . and . . . again —unless we overcome or reduce our vulnerability by better self-management and by preventive techniques.

Anxiety attacks may come and go without much warning. Try as we might at first, we seldom know when to expect these attacks

—unless we've doped out the situation responsible for bringing on anxiety—and the less we know what to expect, the harder the anxiety seems to hit us. It seems to come from outside us, when actually it may be our own doing (for the most part); no matter where anxiety comes from it is up to us to undo or control the anxiety.

One person known to the writer developed a tendency to become anxious when in crowds—when crossing a busy street, entering a crowded room or building or elevator. Her anxiety attacks were sometimes so overwhelming as to render her almost helpless —leading her to pull absent mindedly at her hair, to show a vacant stare, and to walk around or retread her steps aimlessly.

This young lady's anxiety lead to an embarrassing situation for her. She was observed anxiously pacing back and forth near the rear entrance of a classroom at her college, and the professor, without knowing her identity, called a security officer because of her apparently "suspicious behavior." She was apprehended by security police as a "suspect" (since there had been threats and break-ins wholly unrelated to this young lady's behavior) and questioned at length. Her behavior, although bizarre, was not likely to involve or injure others, but a superficial view of her actions did not tell the observer or the police what her manner meant. Her behavior therefore aroused fear and apprehension among several people, leading to her considerable embarrassment. Later it was learned she was so distraught she did not know where she was nor what she was doing. One never knows the extent to which consuming anxiety may take its toll!

People's anxieties—if properly catalogued—could fill an encyclopedia! Stories about anxieties people suffer from, and their effects, could fill the stages of all the theatres in the world—each with a different play about anxiety.

In this age of anxiety, relief is needed.

Relief from anxiety might come from a more nearly perfect world. Or it might come from everyone becoming a therapy patient. But who would do the therapy if there were no non-anxious persons around? And who would arrange the "perfect" world?

Surely we do not all need therapy.

Surely we can all help ourselves some, before the perfect world is at hand.

We can do a lot of things for ourselves and others to reduce and prevent common anxieties and their debilitating influences.

This book is about self-help in the face of anxiety. It is a book of tried and valuable methods of handling anxiety, methods used by therapists of all persuasions throughout the world.

These anxiety-reducing and anxiety-managing techniques can help in all but the most paralyzing instances (for example, having to face possible serious injury or death of a loved one).

Each of the methods of anxiety management described here can be applied to a variety of anxiety-provoking situations. However, you have to learn to use the methods judiciously and sparingly. Too much "application" will only inure you to change and even risk making the anxiety worse. It is like taking too much medicine, which not only doesn't help the illness but may make it or the additional side-effects worse.

We are ready now to tackle the anxieties we all experience and learn how to drive these apparent "demons" out of our lives, or at least hush their cries to some extent.

Chapter I

What is anxiety?

Anxiety is a general feeling of *discomfort.*

Do you sometimes feel "boxed-in" because of something you have to do that you don't want to do? Because someone—including yourself—is going to *expect* something from you that you are not sure you can deliver?

The discomfort—the boxed-in feeling—the unsureness . . . the un-fulfilled expectation . . . that's all anxiety. You know it when you feel it, but you don't know what caused it.

This discomfort is partly *physiological,* that is, it involves your body, and partly *psychological,* it is based on the way you think and feel about yourself, and how you can evaluate your experiences.

Some ways in which the discomfort called anxiety can affect your body, or be registered by your body include the following:

Sweaty palms.
Dry throat.
Cracking or hard-to-control voice.
Jitteriness or nervousness.
Clumsiness.
Failure to concentrate the way you usually can.

1

Trouble remembering common things (names, for example, which can cause additional embarrassment and anxiety). Rapid heart beat—shortness of breath.

Also, some people get upset stomachs when anxious. They are bothered by gas or pain in the stomach, may have to go to the toilet very frequently to urinate or may have loose bowel movements.

There is almost no end to the number and type of bodily stress and discomfort that signal anxiety. Your body is your barometer, temperature gauge and pressure gauge when it comes to telling you about anxiety.

Anxiety has *psychological* aspects as well. They intertwine with the physiological ones. When you notice that your body shows stress (sweaty palms, weak voice, stomach upset, etc.), you begin to feel that something serious might be happening to you. You worry about what is going on with your body, maybe for the moment not even recognizing that you are anxious. You may not know how to face the fact that anxiety is the central issue.

If you could say to yourself, "There, I'm anxious about _____," chances are this would help your psychological concern and also relieve some of the bodily stress.

Lots of people think the anxiety that registers itself with rapid heart beats and shallow, quick breathing is due to an impending heart attack or to some "weakness of the heart." People may rush to their physician, take tranquilizers or sleeping pills or aspirin, or anything to relieve the heart's pounding. Chances are it is mainly anxiety that is confronting, confusing and disturbing them, but given these concerns they should get a medical check-up nonetheless.

We often fail to recognize that the psychological aspects (feelings, experiences we call "mental," thoughts, images, etc.) are *interwoven* with the physiological or bodily ones. We "read" the signs of distress as possibly some physical illness (stomach, heart, back, throat), not recognizing that it may well be anxiety that is troubling us, and we may go off into the wrong direction in our effort to remedy the situation.

Anxiety hits us in both ways then—bodily and psychologically—and if we can recognize this and try to cope with the double or dual nature of the problem of anxiety, we can learn to be more successful in controlling it in our daily life. Knowing that anxiety *is* anxiety and acting to control or eliminate it is our first step to better self control, more personal comfort, and assured well-being.

The bodily signs of anxiety derive mainly from the autonomic nervous system. That is the part of our nervous system that is the oldest in terms of the history of the race, the oldest and most primitive in terms of all living animals, including man. The autonomic nervous system is a primitive "signal system" that tells us that danger is at hand, and gives us the energy to fight or to run away and escape. This activity, fighting or escaping, takes more energy than just lolling around or tending to one's business. When some danger triggers the autonomic nervous system, the whole body is put into the business of getting ready for fight or flight, and that is why, when we experience anxiety, there appear so many bodily signs or physiological components.

When you see or sense danger (sound and touch are senses that can signal danger, although in our complex world we rely more on sight for all kinds of adjustment including the recognition of danger), the sense organ involved transmits a message to the autonomic nervous system that some kind of emergency exists. The autonomic nervous system pumps a fluid called *adrenalin* into the blood stream, which helps to make you stronger and more vigorous in the event of activity (fighting or fleeing), helps to make the blood clot (if injured), and generally prepares you for the emergency at hand.

Since these physiological changes do not take place very rapidly, not, for example, as rapidly as *reflexes* such as pulling your hand quickly away from some danger or blinking the eyes when a foreign object comes near, we experience the on-coming of anxiety more slowly, but nonetheless convincingly. Once these physiological changes are activated, they tend to persist overtime. Therefore we may continue to experience the bodily signs of anxiety after the real danger has passed. Even when the danger has passed us by, our bodies do not immediately know this (although our vision or hearing or touching sense may tell us this), so the adrenalin already pumped into our blood stream continues to have the same influence for a while. The body under the influence of anxiety tends to recover slowly.

Not only are the bodily signs of anxiety, signalled as they are by danger, likely to continue for a while, our psychological signs (feelings, thinking, etc.) also continue to be prepared for an emergency. We cannot concentrate on anything but the danger; we do not remember other things because the preparation our bodies have undergone is so compelling as to screen out other considerations; and our breathing, our skin surface, and digestion are still under the influence of the emergency that provoked the anxiety reaction. All of these matters make us glued, so to speak, psychologically to the situation at hand and disallow other interests we may have when we are calm and collected.

Now the body acts as it does because that is the way nature programmed us over the eons of time the human race and its ancestors were evolving. It is the remarkable work of nature that has given the living creature ways to preserve its life, to combat danger and threats to life. If something is a life-and-death matter, it is very important, and so the whole of the body and the mind have to be focused on this very vital issue.

Anxiety, then, is not only a matter of the immediate disturbance at hand for each of us, the immediate interactions between ourselves and others that make us anxious, but is also a matter of how nature set us up long, long ago to deal with anxiety and fear and the emergency situations they arise from. Most of the anxiety-provoking situations that you and I meet in everyday life do not require the prodigious efforts of the body to solve them, but the mechanisms of the body and its workings are nonetheless there to use. We have to learn to cope with the body and its reactions in the face of anxiety, and the effect all this has on each of us as *persons*.

In everyday life, we do not usually meet total emergency situations, although such situations may occur. But our bodies, and indirectly our minds (the psychological aspects), are prepared *as though* we were about to have to cope with a total emergency. That is why, when we are made anxious by what is really a minor situation (although it may be important to us, socially and interpersonally, at the moment), we nonetheless have the whole body thrown into the works by nature as if a total emergency were present.

Nature has not reprogrammed us, so to speak. Nature got us ready for BIG ANXIETY but we do not have to face such issues ordinarily in daily life; our bodies have not been scaled down to the new size we need in order to meet everyday exigencies with less power. It is as if we had to use hammers to kill flies because there was no such thing as a flyswatter!

The Anxiety Chart

Psychological Aspects (Thoughts, Images, Feelings, other "Mental" states)	*Personal Aspects* (Headaches, Pounding Heart, Dry Mouth and Throat)
Physiological Aspects (Person prepared for Flight or Fight)	*The Human Race Aspects* (Prepared by nature to meet life-defying situations)

The Anxiety Chart will show you how the psychological and physiological aspects, together with the personal and whole-human-race backdrop to anxiety, can be brought together in one organized whole. Each person experiences anxiety in relation to these four considerations.

The Psychological Aspects include our thoughts, images, feelings, subjective discomfort states, and our "mental" states. Within the psychological aspects come our own Personal Aspects, those characteristics that each of us experience as anxiety; these may differ from one person to another but include such complaints as headache, pounding heart, dry mouth and throat, sweaty palms, stomach upset, blurred vision, a sick or queasy feeling in the stomach, and so forth.

The Anxiety Chart is further filled out by reference to the Physiological Aspects which refer to the body being prepared to deal with anxiety when it occurs, being prepared for flight or fight by and through the adrenalin pumped into the blood stream. The Human Race part simply points out that this is the way nature has made us or "programmed" our bodies and "minds" over eons of time.

The lesson from the Anxiety Chart is that we acknowledge anxiety to be what it is—psychological or physiological—but we also must learn how it applies to each of us, and how as sensible human beings we have to learn to control and regulate anxiety better for purposes of personal comfort and effectiveness.

ANXIETY IS PERVASIVE

Since anxiety arises to prepare us, in physiological, bodily and psychological ways, as we have seen, this is a *total* kind of preparation we are forced to make. Anxiety is *pervasive*—it doesn't just cover our ability to run faster and longer in the face of danger, or the strength to pound an enemy with our doubled-up fists; it prepares us for all of these things . . . and more. It is as if nature said, "I don't know what specific kind of emergency you may need to meet, Mr. Human Being, so I am preparing you for all kinds of dangers, the worst of possibilities, then you decide how to use this preparation to preserve your life."

The anxiety we feel, including all the bodily signs, is so pervasive and compelling that we often don't know what it was that set off our anxiety. We are so overwhelmed by the preparation we have forgotten to notice what disturbed us. In the case of mankind, when he was evolving along present lines, the emergency situations he faced were with predatory animals, violent acts of nature, and the like. Early man needed all the help he could get from his body, his senses, and his psychology, to meet the adversity confronting him. The pervasiveness of the anxiety or fear reaction was the best preparation nature could provide to insure survival.

Today, however, our anxiety reactions are triggered off by some slur by a friend, some inconvenience others cause us, or by thoughts we have—forward and backward in time—about some possible past, present or future "danger." The "danger" now is usually not life-defying, but simply disturbing or distressing to us psychologically. Yet we are ready for asserting ourselves as if the danger were crucial to life; nature made us that way!

SOME OTHER CHARACTERISTICS OF ANXIETY

But that's not all there is to anxiety! We're just getting started in understanding it. Besides the psychological and bodily aspects, we have noted, it also shows certain other characteristics such as—

Anxiety arises slowly, like the swelling of
dough when heat is applied.

Anxiety seems to slip up on you and hit
you when you least expect it;
it comes from behind, so to speak.

Anxiety hangs on like it doesn't want to go
away until you take special notice
of its presence.

Anxiety dominates your thinking, feeling and acting
(more so if the anxiety is strong).

Anxiety also tends to drive you away from situations
where you've experienced it before;
it acts as a warning that says, in effect,
"Don't go in there. . ." or "Don't deal with him. . ."
or "Don't try that again. . ."

THE PERSONAL AND PSYCHOLOGICAL ASPECTS

Now let us set aside all the business about nature and how human history made us susceptible to anxiety and get back to the *personal* aspects, our own psychological aspects so we can learn to control them better. Something really does happen, however, to cause us anxiety now . . . here and now, although it is not life defying.

Somebody did say or do something to cause us anxiety . . . or maybe we did it to ourselves (remembering the earlier events that triggered anxiety in the past). The anxiety and its reactions are still with us—only the cause has changed.

Because anxiety is so pervasive and elusive—coming seemingly like the fog in from the sea—we have trouble identifying what set off our reactions. So we just suffer, sometimes in silence, sometimes by making ourselves or others miserable. It takes some "doing" to figure out what caused the anxiety reaction, and most of the rest of this book will address itself to these efforts, the coping behaviors needed to reduce, forestall or preclude anxiety.

CONFLICT AND ANXIETY

We must recognize that all of our personal reactions to anxiety are related to conflicts we have with ourselves and with others.

Conflict is central to anxiety. It is very doubtful if one can experience anxiety without conflict; it is equally likely that any conflict of a serious nature will carry with it a load of anxiety.

In order to understand how conflict figures in anxiety, it is important to draw some distinctions between anxiety and fear.

Fear is a one-way street.
Anxiety is a two-way street.

A ferocious animal sends you in the other direction. You fear the growl, the snarl, the rattle, or other sign of danger. You probably do not hesitate to make your departure (assuming, of course, you don't *have* to approach the animal). Likewise, you stay away from precipitious and dangerous heights, turbulent waters, and you hastily get inside away from the lightning and windstorm. Fear responses also include physiological reactions, preparatory for action (fight or flight). The main difference between anxiety and fear is that in the latter case you escape as fast as you can. With anxiety, you are trying to go both ways on a two-way street; you want to approach the area where there is concern, but you doubt your ability to do so . . . you feel you want to and don't want to. Approach is also hampered by avoidance, and so the clash between motives results. That is anxiety—that is conflict!

Let us see how conflict figures more completely in anxiety. You want to give a speech at a meeting of importance to you in your business or social life or professional activities. You also doubt your ability to "carry it off as you would like to do." You want to both appear and speak *and* want to avoid the inconvenience and doubt (please read: *anxiety*). Forces, so to speak, are operating in *both* directions—it is not a unilateral matter like escaping from the rattle snake, attacking bull or burning building.

When you first think about the speech, you revel in it, enjoy the prospect of being noticed, liked, approved-of by others, and perhaps even being agreed-with as to what you plan to say in your speech. But you also think: "What if they don't like me?" "What if I sound stupid?" "What if I don't say anything they don't already know?" And so on through many self-doubts. As the time to speak approaches, the feelings of escape and doubt loom larger and the feelings of potential success and approval tend to diminish. You then feel you would like to ". . . get out of that damned speech." You are overwhelmed with an "I-don't-know-why-I-agreed-to-that. . ." feeling. Things are different at this junction. . . you are consumed with *anxiety.*

What do you do? Some people do back out. Others grit their teeth and go through with it. Some get sick and cop out that way. Some arrange to be ". . . called out of town on an emergency. . ." and escape without any onus being placed on themselves (by others), but they know in their own minds that they are copping out.

Suppose you have to speak with a neighbor about how his child behaved (or misbehaved) at your home when playing with your child. Suppose you think the neighbor's child damaged a valuable article or took something not belonging to him. You have to go over to "Jones," your neighbor, and address the matter with him. You feel you should do it, yet you are very reluctant. Why the two feelings? Why the conflict? First of all, you have circumstantial evidence only relating the neighbor's child to the missing or damaged article. You did not *see* the child commit the alleged injustice. So your evidence is moot. You like the child and the neighbor and you don't want to offend either of them—you don't want to look silly by accusing the child (and indirectly the parent) of something you cannot prove. Yet you hold tenaciously to the idea that ". . . the child must have done it . . . he was the only one here at the time. . ." and so you feel the injustice has to be rectified. Besides, your wife (or husband, or someone) is urging you to ". . . go through with finding out what happened . . . and don't be so Casper Milktoast about it. . . ."

You sweat . . . you fume . . . you mull it over and over . . . you don't sleep . . . you meet Jones accidentally at the gas station and you hardly know how to speak to him . . . and you are mum at home with your wife (or husband) . . . and you just fret and fret and fret. There's no easy solution. You can't drop either alternative. You are in *conflict*. You are *anxiety-ridden*. You are in hot soup! And nobody can tell you what to do . . . and nobody can do it for you. You're stuck . . . and mighty stuck at that! You cuss yourself, the neighbor's child, your own child and anybody else you can think of.

As the poet said,

> *"When you're lying awake with a dismal headache,*
> *and repose is tabooed by anxiety,*
> *I conceive you may use any language you choose*
> *to indulge in, without impropriety."*

Conflict and anxiety-provoking situations are legion. We experience them each day. The matter is that most of them are more or less easily resolved; it is just the formidable ones that hang us up, drain us of energy and make us into unknown selves.

With an anxiety you are currently experiencing that is not easily resolved, take a look at the conflict that undergirds the anxiety. Ask yourself: "What is it I *want* to do?" and "What is it I *do not want* to do?" in regard to the situation about which you are anxious. Once you can identify the *approach toward* and the *retreat from* the conflict situation, you can begin to get a leg up on the problem and move toward a resolution. Otherwise you just stew; and the worst part about the stewing is that the pre-occupation disables you in other ways—you can't concentrate, you can't be joyous, you can't think clearly, you can't function in the manner you ordinarily do.

Conflict has certain features that help to explain what you feel when you are caught in conflict. We have said already that there is an *approach* aspect to conflict, and an *avoidance* (escape, retreat from . . .) aspect. These two features have some differences that are important—

Approach is slow, gradual and moderately elevated.
Avoidance is abrupt, steep and immediate.

These characteristics are depicted in Figure 1.

If a house catches on fire, you escape and get away as fast as you can. The steepness of the Avoidance Gradient illustrates that fact. The Approach Gradient, on the other hand exhibits less urgency, and is a gradual matter. Farther away from the Goal area (this could be interpreted as the time and/or occasion when one would give the speech referred to above), there is consider-ably more Approach; as one nears the Goal area, in terms of time and/or space, the Avoidance Gradient characteristics tend to dominate. This is why our speech giver in the illustration above experiences maximum anxiety as the time and place for the speech approaches.

If there is no anxiety...if there is no conflict, the Approach-Avoidance characteristics do not *both* hold. If the speech-giver has no doubts or concerns, he just goes and gives the speech and that's that! If one escapes from a catastrophe—such as a sinking ship, a burning building, a collapsing bridge—one simply leaves the dangerous situation for safety. There is little or no anxiety in either case if there is no conflict.

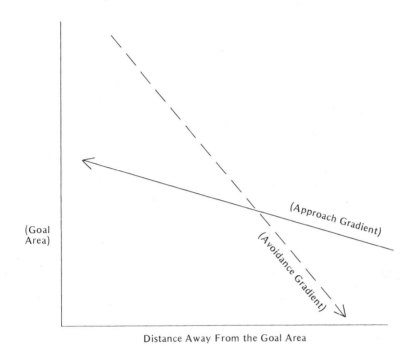

(Goal Area)

Distance Away From the Goal Area

Figure 1. Showing how both Approach and Avoidance work in the case of Conflict. The Approach Gradient is slow and sloping and gradual, the Avoidance Gradient is steep and generally shorter. In the area where the two Gradients cross, one finds the most indecisiveness and inability to take a definite stand.

Now the subtle thing about anxiety and conflict is that, based on our social experiences and our learning, we do not have to have overtly dangerous conditions to excite us; we need to have only our thoughts, or memories of past conflict or anxiety. We carry around in our heads most of the anxiety we experience; we house the conflict in our memory and in our experience, and the whole matter gets reactivated when certain stimuli (or familiar environmental conditions) occur, or reoccur.

This subtle condition allows for some of the apparent mystery of anxiety—we do not always know just what aspect of experience, memory, or our thinking is currently triggering off an anxiety episode. We have to ferret it out; we have to examine our experience carefully to see just what aspects may account for the anxiety. Unfortunately, experiences do not come back to us tagged or labelled; the job of locating the probable cause of the anxiety may not be easy.

The person we talked about above who had to contact a neighbor about his child's involvement in an unsavory situation, had to face the pros and cons of contacting the neighbor; the conflict was relatively open, although probably not well articulated by the person in our example.

Many other conflicts are not as readily apparent or open, many of them are very obscure. The slowness of the anxiety reaction at first, the pervasiveness of the anxiety reaction, and the generally unpleasant feelings associated therewith, all act to make finding the cause difficult. That is why some people spend a lot of time, occasionally unnecessarily, in therapy trying to uncover the earlier origins of their anxiety reactions.

Suppose you are asked by your spouse to accept a dinner engage-ment at Smith's house. You ask who will be there, and maybe some other questions about the prospective evening. You discover that Johnson is going to be there, and you always tend to clash with Johnson (on politics or religion or some topic you hold dear). You demur. You think the dinner at Smith's might be great if Johnson were not going to be there. But just what is there about Johnson that is so powerful that it can keep you away from an otherwise enjoyable dinner party? Is Johnson smarter than you? Does he think of things you do not think of? Is he over-bearing? Does he refuse to listen to what you say? Surely some of these things, or other similar ones, turn you off when it comes to interacting with Johnson—but which ones? If you know more precisely what there is about Johnson that turns you off, you would be onto something important, and possibly able to either preclude an anxiety reaction or reduce it considerably (remember, there's conflict here: wanting to go to the dinner party at Smith's, but being reluctant on account of Johnson's presence there, too). It isn't just that Johnson dis-agrees with you; it is something in the manner in which he disagrees . . . something in the way he undermines you, your argument, your position. His challenge is *personal*, not simply theoretical or topical. Find what that personal element is in your anxiety . . . what is personal about his approach to you, and you have underway a solution to the anxiety.

Take any situation that has anxiety for you. First note that you have to go or do what's required or recommended. You are in conflict with these wishes, you have your reluctances. Pin down these opposing elements. Then you will be a bit more advanced on solving the issue than you otherwise would.

Remember, too, that although you are capable of being in conflict, hence reacting anxiously, with regard to a multitude of things (people, events, circumstances), most likely your anxiety will revolve about some items of personal importance, something relating to self-esteem or self-worth (or self-doubt, which may be at the lower end of the scale in these matters). The anxiety just cannot help touching some personal conflict area of considerable importance to you. The more anxiety you have, the more areas of personal worth are being challenged by events or experiences; conversely, the less anxiety on a continuing basis you experience (we would also have to include acute anxieties) the more you recognize your own stability and personal comfort. The more of one, the less of the other.

Besides the ways we have mentioned above in coping with anxiety there are many other things you can do. The rest of this book will list and discuss a number of these measures. No one measure is perfect; some measures are more for you than others, but all of them work to some extent for most people.

We continue with a discussion of reducing anxiety by developing ASSERTIVENESS.

> STOP NOW and try to remember what you have read. Speak aloud to yourself about the chapter, then look back to check it out.

Re: ANXIETY—YOUR OWN AND THAT OF OTHERS
Things To Observe and Do

1. Note and write down how often you have a conscious anxiety experience *each day*.

	Sunday	Monday	Tuesday	Wednesday	Thursday	Friday	Saturday
1st wk							
2nd wk							
3rd wk							
4th wk							
5th wk							

Circle the ones causing you the most trouble. Do this *before* you go on to the next chapter.

2. Note anxious periods shown by others—in their speech, gestures, the way they look at you and so forth. Try to make the other person more comfortable at these times. For example:

    Monday — John stammered and swallowed his words when he spoke to me. I told him I knew he was upset and to calm down before he talked further.

    Tuesday — My mother and I had a fight over money. I told her I would write down views if she would do likewise.

    Etc.

ADDITIONAL READINGS

I'm OK—You're OK by Thomas A. Harris, M.D., Avon Publisher, New York, 1967.
The Way of Zen by Alan W. Watts, Vintage Books—Random House, New York, 1957.
The Book On Taboo Against Knowing Who You Are by Alan W. Watts, Vintage Books—Random House, New York, 1972.

Chapter II

Reducing anxiety by developing ASSERTIVENESS

Everyone today has heard a lot about assertiveness. Courses, books, lectures, workshops and demonstrations all attest to the popularity of training in assertiveness. Assertiveness is, in a way, at the heart of the movement to liberate women. It is also at the heart of eliminating prejudice against blacks, Chicanos, Mexicans, and, indeed, any minority or oppressed group. When we admonish people to stand up for their rights, we instruct them on how to be assertive.

Assertiveness is equally important for others as well. You don't have to be a member of an oppressed minority group to avail yourself of some of the benefits of asserting yourself more ably. You may simply be just too meek in stores, in dealing with friends and neighbors. You may be easily taken advantage of, easily put down, easily ignored, all to your own detriment.

Assertiveness comes into play for the average person in two important ways:

1. When you are too shy . . . too reluctant . . . too demuring to state what you feel or think. You may not be taken advantage of by others, but you may not act on or obtain a

possible advantage (or even equality) for yourself. You are like the ball player who does not swing forcefully and convincingly when at bat; you don't step up to the plate and swing your mighty best!

2. When you are actually taken advantage of by others, owing to your not stating your own rights, privileges, opportunities. This can occur when you are preempted in line . . . when you are called "out" in the ball game without having been given a chance . . . when others take advantage of you in one or several ways. (Socially and culturally, minority groups are taken advantage of very often in this way, as are poor people, foreigners, and others who do not ". . . know the ropes. . .")

You have to decide which type of situation applies to you. Are you too meek or are you actually being taken overt advantage of? On different occasions, you may be one type, yet in other situations you may be another type.

Assertiveness is stating what you think or feel using *pleasant but firm* action or language. The key words are: pleasant but firm. Assertiveness is not aggressiveness. Assertiveness is not bowling over someone, or taking advantage of another before you get "taken" yourself.

Another word that might do, although it is not in common parlance in this context, is *Ascendance*, "increasing in prospect, influence, authority." One is then rising to the occasion demanded of him; one is asserting (or ascending to) one's own authority to define and deal with a situation (which, of course, is one's right).

DEFINING ASSERTIVENESS

To further define assertiveness, we might use the following:

1. It should be appropriate to the situation.
2. It should not be abrasive or unwarranted.
3. It should reduce your own tendency to feel guilty, or react with anxiety after a given encounter.
4. It should help you avoid producing negative responses in yourself or in others.
5. It should help you develop assurance, conviction, and confidence in the way you speak or behave.
6. It does not involve manipulation or deceit toward others.

7. It is specific to a given situation, but one might then learn to generalize assertiveness to other relevant situations.
8. It has regard for others' feelings and behavior; it does not build on destroying another's position or the feeling of another person (even though the person may act that way toward you).
9. It replaces passivity and meekness with confidence and conviction. (See also Chapter IX in this connection.)
10. It avoids ruminating, worrying, reliving anxiety-provoking situations after they have occurred.
11. It readies a person for future effectiveness.
12. It allows one to set aside his underassertive past and live more effectively in the present.

A popular notion of assertiveness is that people learn how to say "no" when they mean no, and learn to avoid saying "yes" in a similar type of situation. On the "yeses" and "nos" we utter, hang a wide assortment of complications and the possibilities of more gratifying interpersonal relations.

In a mental health sense, we often recognize people who are too self-effacing, too prone to agree or be compliant, and later "blow up" on a slight provocation. We are amazed at the contrast in their personalities, with the apparent inconsistency in their behavior. We occasionally read newspaper accounts about some seemingly gentle person who ends up axing someone. Sometimes the victim of such violence is not even known to the assailant. This is an example of *aggressiveness* gone wild; it is certainly not assertiveness used humanely!

We might, then, think of assertiveness as an antidote to aggressiveness, as shown in Figure 2, below. We might think also of assertiveness as occupying some middle ground between meekness (or passivity) and aggressiveness. In this case, meekness or passivity, under extreme continuing pressure, can give rise to aggressiveness and explosiveness, with the middle ground of assertiveness left out.

Meekness — — — — — — Assertiveness — — — — — — — Aggressiveness
(Passivity)

Figure 2. Showing how Meekness (or Passivity) may explode into Aggressiveness, overshooting the middle ground of Assertiveness. Failure to act Assertively allows one to become more vulnerable to the ills of Passivity and Aggressiveness.

On the other hand, if assertiveness occupies the main position as in Figure 3, below, it tends to balance and absorb the extremes of meekness (or passivity) and aggressiveness, and to preclude the need for both extremes.

Assertiveness

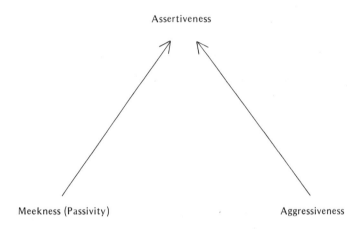

Meekness (Passivity)   Aggressiveness

Figure 3. Showing how Assertiveness can occupy the middle ground between Meekness (Passivity) and Aggressiveness. The purpose of Assertiveness training is to develop and utilize ascendent and assertive approaches to problems and to leave out the extremes of passivity and aggressiveness. (See also Chapter IX which develops the above Figure more fully.)

In this manner, assertiveness tends to avoid the tension build-up from underassertiveness (meekness, passivity) and the resultant vulnerability to explosiveness or aggressiveness. (See Chapter IX for more discussion on this point.)

GUILT

One outcome of not being sufficiently assertive in the face of anxiety is to be subject to guilt and self-recriminations later. These re-criminations are composed of a multitude of "second thoughts." "Why didn't I do that differently?" "Why didn't I see that sooner?" "Why didn't I catch myself before I let that happen?" And so on and so on. This Monday morning quarterbacking will not win any games or solve any problems.

To be assertive is to do the best you can in standing up for your rights, in stating your case, in trying to be fair to yourself and to the other person as well. So long as you do that, you have no reasons for recriminations, no ruminations over past mistakes or future concerns. When you are reasonably and appropriately assertive, you have few or no left-over, unsolved problems. You clear the air and let it go at that; you feel good about the assertiveness and this reinforces your effort and your realism. You are ready for the next encounter with reality, again with appropriate assertiveness and ascendance.

If you feel guilty after an encounter with another person where you have possibly "put it over on him . . . ," or perhaps feel you did not deal candidly with that person, you end up not only with guilt but also with feeling that you have not been honest with yourself. You feel you have let yourself down. And well you have!

The only way you can be honest with yourself—and only you will know whether you have or not—is to be forthright with your own feelings and convey them judiciously to others. One young man in therapy was constantly getting into difficulty with girl friends because he did not deal candidly with them. He tells his story:

"I guess I just don't come on straight with the girls I like. I try to win them over too quickly and not give them a chance to differ with me. I do this by promising too much. . ."

The discussion with this young man continued:

"Well, you see I talk serious talk with them. I make out like I love them a lot . . . and I make promises I think they will like."

Later in the discussion this young man, who continued in therapy, outlined in some more detail how he got into a too-involved situation with one girl he wanted to impress and take to a big prom and weekend affair that was soon coming up.

"You see I wanted to take Jane to this dance and to the whole weekend out in the country after the dance. I let her think I was in love with her when she asked me if I did love her. I felt if I was truthful she would not take me seriously enough to go to the dance and spend the whole weekend with me where a bunch of us were going swimming, hiking, mountain climbing and things like that. I felt I had to put on some extra reasons which was really being dishonest with her."

One of the reasons this young man entered therapy was to help straighten out his relationships with women, and to learn to assert himself with them more honestly and appropriately.

Needless to say, women have equally difficult times asserting themselves. In fact, it is more common for women to be underassertive than for men to be underassertive. Women are "trained" by our culture to be meek and compliant, even when it hurts them, their self-esteem and their pride.

One such woman was Rhonda who felt she could not tell her husband how she felt about things for fear he would get mad at her, ignore her, "put her down" or "tell her off." She would nurse personal wounds for days or weeks before she would bring an important matter to his attention, for fear she would only worsen her plight with him; yet not to speak up was also painful.

Some of the discussion with Rhonda went as follows:

Therapist: You feel you really have to tell him about making those beach arrangements for next month?

Patient: Yes, but I can't get up the courage. . . He will be furious when he learns how much I had to pay for the three-day reservation.

Therapist: How do you think you should go about the matter of informing him?

Patient: Well, I could just blurt it out one day before he leaves for work so he won't have time to get on my back.

Therapist: Or . . .?

Patient: You mean that's not the way to do it?

Therapist: When a person is afraid of asserting him or herself, that person usually looks to subterfuges or round-about ways . . . think that applies to you?

Patient: Yes, it surely does? What *should* I do?

Therapist: What do you want to say . . . what is simply the honest fact?

Patient: That I made an expensive reservation at the beach for 3 days . . .

Therapist: Then why not start there?

Patient: You mean it is just that simple?

Therapist: It is simpler than a "round-about," isn't it?

Patient: Yes, it is, but I am still scared . . .

Therapist: I know you are, but that will remain so until or unless you tell him, and the simpler the telling, the better, it would seem.

Patient: I know how he will feel as soon as I get out the first few words.

Therapist: You could start with his feelings about it . . . "You know, honey, I have to tell you something you may not like . . . I made some reservations at the beach with the Browns that are a bit expensive . . ."

Patient: Yes, that might help to start with an anticipation of *his emotional* reaction. . .

Therapist: You are killing two birds with one stone . . . capturing how he feels first which may ameliorate his reaction some, *and* giving him the facts.

Patient: That sounds so easy when you say it.

Therapist: It will get easier for you with the saying . . .

Patient: Let me see if I have it right. I begin by letting him know he will not like what I am about to say . . .

Therapist: (Interrupting) Correct . . .

Patient: And . . . and . . . then go on to say what I have done— made the expensive reservations.

Therapist: As a matter of interest and fact, why were the reservations "expensive" as you say?

Patient: Well . . . you see . . . we're going with the Browns . . . and they want to be on the water side of the motel . . . and there was only one other apartment left in the rear near a business street . . . so I took the better one and sent half the money for our share of the 3-day weekend costs.

Therapist: So there's really no acceptable recourse now? Well . . . back to the communication with your husband . . . what do you think now? Does this make sense to you? Can you do it?

Patient: I hope so! I'll try . . . it's hard, though.

Therapist: We can't ask for more than that.

In the discussion with Rhonda, there emerged three aspects of her asserting herself with her husband (and possibly with others as well):

1. Approaching the assertive communication via the way the other person *probably* feels about the matter at hand. That is, capturing that person's feelings *at the outset.* This sets the stage, reduces the other person's emotional reaction, and allows the speaker (the one being assertive) to know he/she has approached the doubtful and difficult matter as adroitly as possible at the time.
2. Allows the person being assertive (the one bringing up the difficult matter) to proceed with some confidence.
3. Provides a basis for future follow-up on the issue by having set the stage and having made the assertive approach to the problem. It is then a *problem to be solved,* not just a dangling issue.

In Rhonda's case, the third point here was not discussed in the therapy hour cited above, but it was discussed during the next hour.

Therapist: What, then did your husband say when you carried off this matter so well?

Patient: Well . . . he fumbled some, stuck his hands in and out of his pockets and twisted around some and then said . . . "Well, I guess it's been done and there's no use hacking it over and over."

Therapist: Good show!

Patient: And I was then *greatly* relieved.

Therapist: I'll bet! (Pause) What do you now think of this pleasantly but firmly assertive approach?

Patient: I think it's great! I just hope I can keep it going.

Therapist: All situations calling for assertiveness on your part will not be as easy as this one, likely.

Patient: I know that . . . I'm just thankful that it wasn't any harder.

Therapist: However, you cannot preclude other reactions; you must meet them as they occur. But assertiveness is always needed.

Patient: I'll say it is—especially by *me.*

All of this amounts to the need to be honest with oneself and with others. The young man cited above was not being honest with his girlfriend; Rhonda was trying to be honest with her husband but lacked the courage and skill to do it well. In either case, being circuitous was not going to help, but would only complicate matters and make the next conflict worse.

RESPECTING THE FEELINGS OF OTHERS

Assertiveness begins by being respectful of the other person's feelings too. It is not just a matter of just telling the other one how you stand. Some ways in which being respectful of the other person's feelings may be illustrated as follows:

1. "John, I know you are going to disagree with what I am about to say . . . but I must say it."
2. "Honey . . . even though we've differed on this matter before, and I know how you feel, I need to tell you again how I feel and what I think . . ."
3. "Susan . . . even though it pains both of us to talk about this matter, I must bring it up in relation to . . ."
4. "Even though we differ on this matter, Ken, we have to bring it up again because of the children . . ."
   And so forth . . .

In these instances, one is beginning where the other person is *at* and going on from this important starting point to meet the issue. This approach respects the other one's view, acknowledges previous discussions, and recognizes a real difference in opinion or outlook. There is no greater fairness where major difference exists than in proceeding in this manner.

Assertiveness solves problems, or moves them toward solution, without which anxiety would prevail and continue. As we have noted in the first chapter, anxiety derives from conflict between two opposing tendencies or motivations. Assertiveness helps to acknowledge the conflict—"You know, Sam, we've discussed this before and I know you differ with me . . . but . . ."—and allows the to-be-assertive person to develop an approach to the conflict. It gives some promise, if the assertiveness is appropriate, to a resolution or amelioration of the problem.

The reason anxiety continues in some situations is that nothing different happens. In the case of Rhonda, above, if she had not developed a new way of approaching her husband, the anxiety and discouragement she felt would continue to this day . . . and longer. Some new inputs are needed, and they are inputs that move steadily, through assertiveness, to direct handling of the anxiety. Anxiety, also, as we have noted, tends to drive one away from the situation that calls for solution, so that if all that is learned is how to escape the unpleasantness one is facing, the anxiety will never be challenged. Hence it will prevail.

Assertiveness is not always easy to employ. People who have been unassertive tend to overdo it (become *over*-assertive) when they first approach a change in their behavior. It is as if they moved from one extreme to another, not recognizing or utilizing any middle ground.

This may be illustrated by the case of Helen:

Patient: You see I read this book on assertive training and I thought I got a lot out of it . . . but I was disappointed when I tried out some of the ideas.

Therapist: I see—can you give me an example of what you mean?

Patient: Well, I guess I had a lot of trouble with a girlfriend of mine who used to call me each day at the absolutely worst time of day . . . and keep me on the phone when I had to get dinner ready or take care of the kids or other things.

Therapist: You had no effective way of handling that?

Patient: Boy, you can say that again!

Therapist: What, specifically, did you find yourself doing in this bind?

Patient: Well, before I read the book I just hung on and on and occasionally tried to get off the phone but wasn't very success-ful (pause) . . . I guess I could be kept on the phone by Donna, my neighbor, for as long as an hour . . . right up to supper time when all hell breaks loose.

Therapist: Did you find any techniques useful in handling Donna?

Patient: Well, if one of the kids screamed because he got hit on the head by the other, I would have to drop the phone and go to the rescue, but I would usually go back to the phone and the conversation—and Donna would wait patiently—and pick up on the conversation.

Therapist: You were telling Donna by your behavior that you wanted to continue the talk, weren't you?

Patient: Yes, I was . . . but I didn't see that *then.*

Therapist: When did you see that?

Patient: After I read the book on assertive training.

Therapist: And just what instruction did you then receive?

Patient: That I was probably guilty when I thought of cutting off the phone call . . . and that I felt she wouldn't like me or call me or go places with me. I felt trapped.

Therapist: You were experiencing a conflict between wanting to please Donna and please yourself.

Patient: Exactly! You couldn't say it better!

Therapist: After the reading of the book . . . what then?

Patient: Well, I guess I got nasty with Donna . . . I did tell her off. (Pause) And it hurt both of us.

Therapist: What did you actually say to Donna?

Patient: I said, "Look, Donna, you don't consider my time . . . you always call me at the *worst* time of day and I wish you wouldn't . . ." And then she hung up on me!

Therapist: And . . .

Patient: And I called her back . . . crying and sobbing . . . and very upset and she wouldn't talk to me at all . . . I was heartbroken because I really like her otherwise.

Therapist: You feel you came on too hard in your assertiveness?

Patient: I didn't originally think so, but now I do . . . in retrospect. I guess I must. Also, I saw Donna in the store a few days later and I finally got her to talk with me a little bit . . . (pause) . . . she cried there, said I was cruel and that she didn't mean to annoy me, that she was being friendly and interested . . . and I know she was, basically . . . and so it was just a mess and I felt so terrible.

Therapist: Well intended moves sometimes really end up badly.

Patient: That sure happened to me!

Therapist: What do you now think . . . and what can we address ourselves to?

Patient: I'd like to understand better what I did with Donna . . . what or how I can state my feelings to somebody who seems at first not to listen until they are bowled over.

Therapist: Are you trying to reconstitute your relationship with Donna?

Patient: I'd like to . . . but I don't know if she would.

Therapist: How would you approach her—start with that practical situation—how would you make a move toward her if you wanted to get the relationship going again?

Patient: I think I would call her and apologize? And try to see her face to face.

Therapist: Have you tried that?

Patient: No.

Therapist: Are you likely to?

Patient: Yes, I'm just getting up courage, I think.

Therapist: How do you plan—give me some detail—how do you plan to go at this?

Patient: Well, I'll call her and ask her if I can come by.

Therapist: If she says "yes," then that's a start. If she says "no," where are you?

Patient: Well, I don't know . . . I think she will agree though.

Therapist: Let's assume that—what then?

Patient: I'll go over to her house—she lives about 6 blocks away—and maybe take the kids along, say when I am about to go shopping.

Therapist: And what will you say?

Patient: I'll apologize.

Therapist: Well, what does that mean? Specifically? And how will you say it?

Patient: I'll tell her I am sorry I was so abrupt and that I was upset with the pressures I was under with the kids . . . and I guess just a bunch of excuses.

Therapist: Maybe they are more excuses—excuses that free yourself —than they are efforts to take it first from where Donna is . . . (Pause) See what I mean?

Patient: You mean I'm talking about how *I* feel, now how *she* feels.

Therapist: Exactly!

Patient: How should I begin then?

Therapist: What occurs to you?

Patient: What occurred to me was to apologize and tell her I am sorry—what more is there, really?

Therapist: Lot's more—she's in the same boat you're in—hurt, emotional, regretful, confused, and all that . . .

Patient: You really meant it, or meant me to say it, when I said I should begin with how *she* feels?

Therapist: Yes, if you want to do what you said you wanted to do. (Pause) What occurs to you?

Patient: I guess I could say something like, "Donna I know you are terribly upset with me and I know how I was so abrupt and hurt your feelings . . ."

Therapist: A good start! Bravo!

Patient: You mean it is just like that . . . that's all there is to it? (Pause) Don't you think I'm catering to her and ignoring myself and my feelings?

Therapist: Maybe . . . for the moment . . . but if people are very hurt or angry with you, aren't you of necessity going to start with their feelings if you want to make amends?

Patient: I guess so . . . but I just never thought of it that way. I guess I am too self-centered . . . especially when I'm emotional.

Therapist: And all of us are . . . but if we want to change something that is important to us . . . we begin, don't we, by making the adjustment or change first in ourselves.

Patient: I guess you have something there . . . I just didn't think of it that way.

Therapist: Let's say you're asserting that you want to amend the relationship with Donna, but there is a better way to do it—begin by acknowledging *her* hurt, *her* upset. That's a fact, isn't it?

Patient: It sure is.

Therapist: Asserting yourself doesn't mean you impose your feeling on her, but means *you* begin by asserting that *she* has an upset which you are trying to amend, so you begin with this fact, then go on to the details of the misunderstanding between you.

Patient: I see the fact is—what I should say is—not that I'm upset but that she is . . . and so that is the prime issue.

Therapist: Sure. You could apologize and let it go at that . . . but that wouldn't go very far, emotionally speaking.

Patient: I see . . . I know we'd have to get to that! Boy, that's important . . . and it has me sweating already.

Therapist: It is hard, I know.

Patient: So I begin by saying to her that I know she is upset and angry with me and my behavior and I want her to know that I realize this . . . and hope we can talk it over and work out something.

Therapist: Isn't that a lot better than a superficial apology—you didn't just spill some catsup on her dress on a picnic . . .

Patient: (Laughs) Yeah, that's right!

Yes, to be assertive you must first take the actual situation, as best as you can see it, into consideration. You must begin there, because that is the emotional hole you are in—you can't wish yourself out of it.

Having then asserted that the emotional impasse, or conflict, or anxiety-provoking situation is what it is, you go on to do the work of putting the parts back together again. This may take some time, may require additional assertiveness and perseverance, and may not be easy. But it must be done if good and satisfying and lasting results are to be obtained.

BUT . . . Assertiveness Can Sometimes Be Difficult . . .

The first lesson to learn about assertiveness is that it can work well for you, particularly if you have been an underassertive (or overassertive) person mostly in the past. However, there are some extenuating circumstances which are cited and discussed below, and about which you must give some consideration, because recognition of the extenuating conditions can help you to use assertiveness more advantageously.

In situations involving extreme *authority* (the traffic cop, the judge in the courtroom, a speaker on a platform, a person angry enough to injure you), there has to be extreme caution taken before the usual lessons concerning assertiveness can be implemented. A person who is about to rob you can hardly be dealt with in the usual assertive way. You cannot challenge the minister who, when giving a sermon, seems to you to take undue advantage of the listeners in his congregation (especially yourself in some particular way). Nor can you assert yourself to an angry

traffic officer even though you know, and can ultimately prove
yourself to be, innocent of wrong doing. (You get your chance
later to do your best assertive work about your innocence.)
Most efforts at normal assertiveness in these more extreme
authoritarian situations will be taken as aggressiveness, not as an
assertion of your rights and privileges. Don't then, forfeit the
opportunity for later assertiveness due to poor timing and to
having your efforts grossly misunderstood!

Then, too, extreme *emotional situations* can cause your usual assertive tendencies to go hay-wire, to end up being aggressiveness, or
to render you sputtering and incomprehensible in your efforts
to defend your rights. When you are extremely angry or upset,
assertiveness in the cooler, more effective versions tend to
go-out-the-window and you fail on all counts. Better to first
calm yourself, or wait for a later opportunity to express yourself. Emotions cause us to misdirect our energies—we're mostly
ready for a fight or for flight—and not for effective ground-
standing and dispassionate discourse. If you have a tendency
to become emotionally wrought where you should learn to
be assertive, you may first have to get over the proneness toward emotional upset; *then* you can learn assertiveness in its
more effective versions. Piling assertiveness artificially on top
of an emotional upset will only make you look more ineffec-
tual; it will not clear the emotional air, nor will it lead to prob-
lem-resolution.

Genuinely "gray areas" of conduct may make assertiveness difficult,
also. Some of these problems have been discussed elsewhere
(see Chapter VI). For example, what "rights" do both smokers
and non-smokers have in a variety of social situations? Sometimes rules in one's household can take care of the matter. "We
prefer that you don't smoke at the table, but it's all right in the
living room," the host might say, or rules in public places,
"Smoking at the rear of the bus only," the sign might say. But
these are exceptional and fairly clear-cut situations; many others
are not so clear. What if one is smoking a seat or two from you
at a lunch counter and blows smoke in your face? What about
drivers taking advantage of you as a pedestrian when they are
turning a corner? What about common situations in dormitories
where some people play their hi-fi sets too loudly or too late in
the evening for the comfort of others? Institutional rules are
often needed to really solve these kinds of problems; individual-
level assertive efforts may not only not be clear as to "rights

and privileges" of the parties involved, but may, indeed, add such complication to the interpersonal impasse that a solution at the time is rendered impossible. Backing off for the time, reasserting one's feelings to the appropriate persons (the manager of the lunch counter might be persuaded to erect a "non-smoking" sign) might be the better route to go, rather than falling back on an unassertive role which says, "Oh, let it go—it doesn't happen too often and it might not happen again, although it is pretty bad to have to eat choking on someone else's smoke."

If all this complication bothers you too much, just relax a bit.

We turn now to seeing how Relaxation can be of help too. We need all the help we can get in handling anxiety, and relaxation is another tool in our kit.

> **RECITE** to yourself the main points in the chapter; think of ways you can now act on the information to aid assertiveness.

Re: ASSERTIVENESS

Things To Do

1. Jot down two to three situations in which you've not been assertive. Then, next to these, jot down how you might have been more assertive.

    (a) I let Sam talk me into having a beer after work and I got home late for supper and made my wife mad.

    (a′) I could have told Sam I'd take a rain check and have a beer another time with him.

    (b)

    (b′)

    (c)

    (c′)

ADDITIONAL READINGS

Don't Say Yes When You Want to Say No: How Assertive Training Can Help You by Herbert Fensterheim, David McKay Co., New York, 1975.

TM—Discovering Inner Energy and Overcoming Stress by Harold Bloomfield, Michael Cain and Dennis Jaffe, Delacorte Press, New York, 1975.

Own Your Own Life by Richard Abell with Cloris W. Abell, David McKay Co., New York, 1976.

The You That Could Be by Fitzhugh Dodson, Follett, Chicago, 1976.

Creative Coping: A Guide To Positive Living by Julius Fast, Morrow, New Jersey, 1976.

Scripts People Live: Transactional Analysis of Life Scripts by Claude M. Steiner, Grove Press, New York, 1974.

Chapter III

Reducing anxiety by relaxation

Relaxation is one of the greatest antidotes to tension and anxiety that exists. In fact, relaxation is the *opposite* to anxiety: If you are relaxed, you are not anxious; if you are anxious, you are obviously not relaxed.

Any time you can face up to the need to relax when you notice you are anxious or tense, you are at least partly on the road to better handling of anxiety. People who lie down for a nap, take a breather, go out and walk around—do any number of things to promote relaxation—are doing themselves a service that is very important in handling the emotional clutches we all face.

Relaxation is important for three basic reasons:

To get over immediate tensions and anxieties.
To prepare one's self for new problems that may come up.
To prepare for future assertiveness that is less hampered by anxiety.

Relaxation in the face of tension engendered in contact (and conflict) with others may include the following informal procedures you can readily use.

1. Dismiss yourself from the tension momentarily. Go get a

drink of water, make a phone call, bend over to tie your shoe, go to the bathroom . . . anything to break the immediate impasse. These little self-imposed breaks give you time to get a new perspective on something . . . they are a bit like "counting ten . . ." and thereby gaining time. You don't leave the tension-provoking situation permanently, but only long enough to get a second wind.

2. In the case of anxiety provoked in adversity with others, repeat to your adversary what was just said. Say, "If I understand you correctly . . . you are saying that I . . ." This lets the other person know you understand *his* argument or his way of contesting, but does not force you to take a strong stand at the time yourself. You are a bit mad, tense or anxious owing to the discussion thus far, but you are really in a better condition to repeat what your opponent has said. When he answers that you have indeed understood his point, you have subtly reduced his power or argument or persuasiveness and have gotten a short leg up on the problem between you and him. You gain an advantage by being mindful of his position, and thereby reduce *your* tension and his argument. Nothing could be more effective than that!

2. Say to your opponent that you acknowledge *some part* of his argument. Join forces with the opponent to a limited extent, but hold on to other differences that represent what you think or that seem to be in your favor. In fact, you take a tactical position that seems to yield a bit in order to gain a larger strategic advantage. That lowers your tension in this kind of interpersonal situation and better prepares you for the rest of the discussion or argument or whatever other difference exists.

These ways of relaxing in the face of anxiety and tension in interpersonal conflict are extremely helpful, and are often used by sales people, by teachers, by parents, by lawyers, and by others who have to play adversary roles. If they are good for these "professionals" who have to deal with interpersonal conflict at a high level—and very frequently—they will work for you too.

WHOLE BODY RELAXATION PROCEDURES

Many relaxation needs you have aren't necessarily based on immediate conflict with others. Most are in the privacy of your own thoughts and tensions. Relaxation may be engaged in private. That is, you may need to develop a whole *relaxation procedure* that can help you reduce more generalized tensions and anxieties than are referred to above, and involve your whole body and your emotions/feelings/thinking.

When there is a need for *total bodily relaxation*, you may follow a procedure somewhat like the following one, outlined in a way that you can easily use on yourself.

The directions take the following characteristics.

1. Lie down or lean back restfully in a chair, on a couch, or on a bed. Put feet flat on the floor if sitting in a chair.
2. Close your eyes. This act, alone, is very relaxing.
3. Think to yourself: "I am going to relax as much as I can." Be convinced that you are ready to relax.
4. Raise your arms high above your head as if you were reaching to unscrew a ceiling light bulb. Hold your arms up so that you feel tension throughout your arm, shoulders, and upper torso. Then drop your arms to your side and notice the difference between the tense (reaching) state and the relaxed one.

   (You need to contrast tension with relaxation to better appreciate what tension is and what relaxation is; put them side by side, so to speak, to better bring both tension and relaxation under your own voluntary control, and note how both—tension and relaxation—affect your body, first with the arms, later with other parts of the body. Repeat the effort after a brief rest.)

5. Push your arms out in front of you as if you were "strong arming" someone in front of you. Hold the stance, note the tension in all parts of your arms and shoulders, then relax. Rest a minute and repeat the effort.
6. Do as many different exercises as you can think of with your arms, in all directions from your body—up, down, sideways, always contrasting tension and relaxation, and ending with the relaxed state.
7. Rest for a minute and think about the tension and relaxation experiences you have just produced for yourself.
8. Next, concentrate on your head and carry out a number of tension-relaxation maneuvers with this part of your body. For example, turn your head to the left, or right, as far as you can, and hold the turn for a few seconds, noting the

tension . . . then turn your head back to a forward view and rest momentarily before turning in the opposite directions.

9. Likewise . . . turn your head upward, hold it, note the strain . . . then relax. Look downward, hold the position, note the tension, then relax. Do this several times, but not at too rapid a rate, then relax. Think over what you have noticed about your body.

10. Use your facial muscles next to induce tension and relaxation. There are many little exercises you can employ here: squint your eyes; hold them tightly closed, then relax, again noting the contrast between tension and relaxation. Do similar exercises with a frown, with a tensing up of your forehead; and if you can do it, tense your scalp in a similar way. In all events, bring on the tension deliberately, note the feeling of tension, then relax. Always enjoy the relaxation part of the exercises in each case, and always note how the body responds to the tension-relaxation rhythm you are producing in yourself.

(Don't do the tension-relaxation exercises absentmindedly, or while you are listening to the radio, or talking to someone, or working on a problem. *Concentrate entirely* on what you are doing to and with your body, and let each part of the exercise—tension and relaxation—register itself indelibly on your awareness, supported as it is by the bodily components. Neither the bodily components nor your concentration should be done separately, both need strong and full cooperation for you to get the most out of the effort.)

11. If you feel strained or very tired at this point, stop the relaxation and turn your attention elsewhere for a while. Relaxation should be relaxing, not a chore, not an exhausting effort. If you feel ready to go on to more relaxation efforts, begin with the legs and stretch, bend and extend them similar to the way you did your arms, always leisurely, thoughtfully enough to get the most out of the exercise. Rest between different exercises, and always note clearly the differences between bodily tensions and relaxation states.

12. If you wish to go on to other exercises, concentrate next on breathing. Begin by sucking in as much air as you can . . . fill the lungs to capacity . . . hold the air . . . then let it go. Think of your lungs as a basketball bladder that you fill (by inhaling) as full as you can, keeping the tightness for a

while, then letting go as if the basketball bladder had been punctured, letting the air out all at once. Do not move too hastily with the inhaling and exhaling as you may take in too much air too fast causing what is called "hyperventilation" which gives you a feeling of dizziness and maybe loss of equilibrium; the latter coming from a decrease in the carbon dioxide in the blood. Again, the effort should always be followed leisurely.

13. Sometimes people prefer to use the deep breathing part in between other bodily tension-relaxation exercises. Probably for most people, the deep breathing is the single most relaxing exercise and so they intersperse it between other relaxation exercises with other parts of the body.

The whole exercise, using several or all parts of the body, as illustrated, will probably not take more than 8-10 minutes. If your time is much shorter than that, you may be rushing things too much, hence engaging in artificial, not thoughtful, production of tension-relaxation. If you are taking a lot more time, you may be approaching the wearing and wearying end of the tension-relaxation continuum. You can find your own pace in a few sessions and be comfortable with a fairly constant effort that produces the desired result.

When you have finished the tension-relaxation exercises on a given occasion, rest for a few minutes before taking up your regular activities.

You may want to do these exercises several times a day: before you get out of bed in the morning, sometime during the morning (especially if you anticipate a tense meeting or interview or interaction with another person), perhaps after lunch, a time or two during the afternoon, and certainly again in the evening, especially before going to sleep. The tension-relaxation exercise, many report, prepares them well for sleep, such that sleeping pills, drinking and utter fatigue are not needed.

Some people can get by with a few exercises each day—perhaps one in the morning, one in the afternoon and one again at night. Others need several more sessions per day, especially at first until they get into a frame of mind where they can produce the relaxation they desire with reduced effort and application.

There are, of course, many other exercises you may engage in. Consult any good physical therapy guide book for additional examples. You should always remember, however, that the tension-relaxation exercises are to teach relaxation, not calisthenics nor muscle building!

You need not lie on a bed or a couch to perform the relaxation procedures, although total reclining is probably beneficial to a more nearly complete relaxation for most people. However, you should be mindful of other competing stimuli in the environment when practicing relaxation (others talking, radio and TV noises, bright lights, etc.) and not let the environment compete too much with you when you are trying to relax.

WHEN TO RELAX

The question comes up as to when to relax in the face of an upcoming tension-producing occasion you can clearly anticipate. Many people get tense in meetings with other associates in connection with their work, especially if they have to make reports, answer questions or present evidence to others. In such cases, it is better to prepare in advance for the relaxation effort and not wait until the actual tension-provoking situation is at hand. It is too late then to try to relax; and if you then try so late in the game, both the relaxation effort and the later performance under pressure will likely suffer.

When you are preparing for a given tense occasion, it is better to try several times to relax while thinking about the tension-provoking situation. For example:

Take in a deep breath, hold it, and as you relax, say to yourself, "Relax," and at the same time exhale. Try to picture for yourself the exact tension-raising situation, and as you exhale try to see yourself as relaxed in the real situation. As you exhale, try different statements silently to yourself: "I'm relaxing," "I don't feel tense anymore," "I know this situation won't bother me if I'll relax," and try to discover if any particular verbal formula works best for you.

Try, then, to couple the actual breathing and the whole bodily effort with the silent language related to relaxing that you say to yourself. In this way, you get the optimal benefit from all the relaxation procedures. Remember, always, relaxation is the opposite to tension and anxiety, and the more you experience relaxation—in whatever form—under your own control, the better for you.

COMMON SITUATIONS INVOLVING ANXIETY

Here are a number of common situations in which anxiety prevails. In each instance suggestions for relaxation procedures are offered. You should try them out, modify them when needed, and develop a repertoire of readily available techniques of value to you in the face of any recurrent anxiety provocation you may experience. In the event of *predictable* recurrent anxiety-provoking situations—like taking tests, being interviewed by supervisors, holding positions on committees where you have to report orally to others—you may develop some fairly "pat" techniques that will assist you. When you face unpredictable anxieties—a bawling out by a policeman, anger from a friend, facing the bank examiner, hearing about the cost of house or auto repairs—you have less to go on, but the extent to which you have already coped with anxiety reactions will give you some advantage in meeting these unwelcome situations.

1. *Taking Tests.* Of course you should study and know the material; anxiety reduction will not offset a lack of knowledge! Having studied well, practice several deep breathing exercises beginning a day or so before the test—begin long enough prior to the scheduled time so that you feel comfortable with what you are doing. As you exhale, say to yourself, "I'll concentrate on the test, be relaxed and do my best." Never say to yourself that you shouldn't be anxious; admit the anxiety and begin to bring it under control that way. Having begun well before the test time to practice relaxation, try one or two more relaxation sessions just before the test to add some more composure to your situation. During the test, also, try to stop a minute if you feel you are too tense, sit back, take a deep breath or two, then resume the test. If you have a chance to go to the actual room where the test is given, do that; sit down in a chair you are likely to later occupy, go through enough of the relaxation routine to feel comfortable. Do that a time or two on different days prior to the test date. *Before* you hand in the test stop again for a short time, relax with a deep breath or two, then go back over the exam to see if you want to change anything (this effort will, of course, vary considerably if your test is an objective, short-answer type vs. an essay test). If your test is *oral*, it is very important that you rehearse, under relaxation control, any and all aspects of the testing situation:

Talk aloud to yourself, go to the room where the test will be conducted (if possible); even record your voice on a tape recorder if possible. The more you can hear, and constructively criticize your own voice, the better for you. Relaxation practice before making a tape record is very useful, so that you minimize the strain in your whole body and particularly any strident oral delivery you may ordinarily display when talking under conditions of tension.

2. *Being Interviewed by a Supervisor.* This goes for any interview where you are being assessed—applying for a job, being questioned about your work, being considered for a raise, giving an "exit" interview as you leave a job. Again, the setting in which the interview is to be conducted should be encountered, if possible, with relaxation practice conducted in the situation. Failing that, sit down in an interview-type situation, talk out loud to your hypothetical interviewer, and answer and pose questions in a mock interview. If you have a friend who can orally conduct a mock interview with you, enlist his/her help and invent as many questions as you think you will need to answer. Do the mock interview on several occasions if possible. If you note anxiety in the practice interview, stop, practice relaxation, regain composure, and then resume the interview. Always try to cope with any anxiety before, during or after the interview with relaxation practice. Get to the anxiety and bring it under control as soon as you can. Also, if you know the person who is really going to interview (assess, judge, etc.) you in the real life situation, try to get informal interactions with him/her before the evaluation interview, possibly at a coffee break, informally in the elevator, or any place. Study your reaction to this informal encounter and use relaxation procedures to steady the lack of self control you may think you noted.

3. *Holding Position on Committees Requiring Oral Presentations.* Almost everyone serves on a committee at some time or another and has to make a presentation or official report to the committee or to the organization. With many people, these reports are frought with anxiety—heart pounding, dry throat, weak voice, sweaty palms, fidgety behavior—which leads to embarrassment and self-consciousness. You can practice relaxation prior to the time of the official report and of course go to the actual place where the report is to be rendered, speaking out loud the whole report if possible.

If that is not feasible, you can record your report on a tape, play it back, listing strong and weak spots, and correcting as needed. Relaxation practice before the recording—as mentioned above—is desirable as it prepares you for the composure needed for a confident report. You can also give your report to another member of the committee over a cup of coffee, going over the essentials in an organized way and noting the tension or relaxation accompanying this informality. Using notes and facts to support the report—which is really just being prepared—is also important; anxiety will not be overcome if you are basically ill-prepared and/or disinterested.

Many informal situations may also stir up your anxieties. You can not usually prepare easily for these exigencies, but once they are encountered, you can then engage in the relaxation practice. Often, even in unexpected anxiety-provoking situations, you have some time to get relaxed before meeting the worst. If you know that relaxation exercises are of value, then time and place can be found to engage in them. It is more a matter of having ready tools that can be employed than it is finding a perfect time and place to relax (although that is great if it is available). In summary, some general relaxation guidelines may be recommended.

1. Start relaxation procedures with the easiest-for-you part of the body; then go on to other parts of the body.
2. While most people get most benefit from deep breathing exercises, people still differ in this respect. Some deep breathing is usually recommended, and it may be interspersed between other tension-relaxation exercises.
3. Relaxation should be practiced several times a day.
4. Try subjectively to encompass a picture or image of the tension-provoking situation as you engage in the relaxation procedure. Especially with deep breathing, the exhaling should be accompanied by silently thinking words or phrases of relaxation tied to the situation you are preparing for.
5. The relaxation procedure is no better than your honest effort to make it work—it cannot be hurried or done while you are competing with the relaxation by building up tension in another way (e.g., watching an exciting ball game on TV, or the like).

6. Relaxation practice should have an immediate effect—you should feel the composure very soon after starting. If this is lacking, you are not relaxing sufficiently or you may be distracted by other things.

Some ways in which relaxation can be helped by knowing your own subjective state (your imagery) will be addressed in the next chapter.

TAKE A BREAK, relax, and try to remember what you have read about relaxation. Apply this information to your daily life.

Re: RELAXATION

Things To Do

1. Make a chart for your *daily* relaxation practice. Write in the number for each day, each week.

	Sunday	Monday	Tuesday	Wednesday	Thursday	Friday	Saturday
1st wk							
2nd wk							
3rd wk							
4th wk							
5th wk							

2. Note how anxiety has been reduced by relaxation practice in the following situations (you name them).

   (a) "Relaxed, called Bob, carried on conversation."
   (b)
   (c)
   (d)

ADDITIONAL READINGS

How To Be Awake and Alive by Mildred Newman and Bernard Berkowitz, Random Press, New York, 1975.

The Relaxation Response by Herbert Benson, William Morrow Co., New York, 1975.

How To Make It With Another Person by Richard B. Austin, MacMillan, New York, 1976.

The Hazards of Being Male by Herb Goldberg, Nash, New York, 1976.

Sense Relaxation Below Your Mind by Bernard Gunther, Collier Books, New York, 1968.

You Must Relax, A Practical Method of Reducing the Stress of Modern Living 4th edition, by Edmund Jacobson, McGraw Hill, New York, 1957.

Progressive Relaxation: A Manual for the Helping Professions by Douglas Berrestein, Research Press, Champaign, Illinois, 1973.

Relax and Enjoy Life: Scientific Body Control by William Miller, A. S. Barnes, New York, 1951.

Chapter IV

Imagery
("It's in your head")
and anxiety

You have read that anxiety management is a tricky and formidable problem and in this light you need all the help you can get. What you think, the images that exist "in your head," (this is not literally true, but is only a common manner of speaking) are ways of assessing how anxiety bothers you. Also the study of images in relation to anxiety help you prepare ways to combat the anxiety. Sometimes you get a first look at anxiety through your own thinking, feeling or emoting, and the visual imagery involved.

WHAT IS AN IMAGE?

An image is a "picture" you have of yourself, another person, a relationship, a place, an event. You can draw up an image as a child sitting on your father's lap; or eating mother's cherry pie on a hot summer day; or the greeting of an attractive school teacher as you entered the classroom. You often think about your experiences in terms of images that are repeated, examined, enjoyed, distressed-over, and the like. If we took images away, we would all be less human and less interesting. Images serve both positive and negative purposes; sometimes they are a problem for us and we want to get rid of unpleasant ones; at other times they are cherished and relished for their positive memory-value.

Each of us knows his own image only. You cannot know another person's image—the outsider knows about the image of you (the other person) only through your verbal report.

In spite of these intriguing and limiting aspects of images, talking about them, using them in therapy, employing their value in trying to combat anxiety, are all possible. In fact, these uses of imagery are more than simply possible; they are important aspects of controlling anxiety and making your thoughts and images work for you and not against you.

POSITIVE AND NEGATIVE IMAGES

When you experience anxiety, it is usually accompanied not only by the bodily signs you read above in earlier chapters, but the anxiety is also accompanied by positive and negative images. You see an image of yourself as distressed, as fumbling, as looking or acting "dumb," when you are anxious about making a speech, or asking (in conflict) another person for a favor, or the like. You convey to yourself in the imagery a kind of snap shot of how you feel and how you view the troublesome and anxiety-provoking situation. This imagery thus used, is a negative factor—it works against you in that it allows you to picture yourself, *to yourself,* and, indirectly, to others, as inadequate and bumbling. The imagery may, unfortunately, get to be a habit if you fail too often in some trying situation, and it may reinforce, inadvertently, your negative view of yourself (at least in the situation under which anxiety occurs). You seldom realize until you stop to analyze it how much your imagery influences your behavior (even though that imagery, itself, grew out of earlier overt experiences), and how much you believe unquestioningly what your images tell you. People treat them naively and overlook using images in more positive light (which will be gone into below).

One reason images are important is that you use them as the vehicle for anticipating success or failure. When somebody broaches a topic or activity to you about which you have some misgivings, you immediately conjure up an image of yourself which is largely or wholly negative and you decline the "invitation." If, on the other hand, you are asked to do something you can do, you visualize (use imagery) a success story.

If you had a recording device to tell all that is going on with yourself during any period of time, you would get a small slice of imagery that would spell out your reaction to the world about you, especially in a situation that called up some strong emotional (positive or negative) reaction. If you learn to "read" this imagery accurately, you can gain some value therefrom and prepare yourself better for the task of coping with anxiety and tension. Noting the calibre of the imagery, you can then go on to assertiveness, relaxation, or other ways of coping with the anxiety. It is as if the imagery were the entry point in dealing with anxiety.

Much of the anxiety we are talking about is a matter of *anticipation.* It is often said that "anticipation is greater than realization," meaning that the imagery of what you might do (good or bad) is perhaps exaggerated or augmented, compared to the realization. If you know that you tend to exaggerate in anticipation of some result, you then learn to adjust to this fact, or to adjust downward the exaggerated anticipation. One such illustrative example was noted in the therapy with a 35 year old male, Luke.

Luke's problem was that he could not keep a job very long. Each time he began a new job, he built it up to such heights that no one would have recognized the job as a real one. He imagined, expected, aspired to be a resounding success, such that no one in history could have matched him. It mattered little whether his new found job was waiting tables, selling second-hand cars, checking out groceries in a supermarket, he was out to be—in his private aspirations and images—a world beater. One of his fantasies was that of being accorded a plaque for checking out the most groceries (the highest dollar registration on the cash register) in history. Another was that of selling more cars for more money in a month's time than anyone else on record. He began his imagery of himself in these new (to him) job situations not with a reading of the job and other practical issues (how much he would *really* make, his hours of work, any benefits accruing on the job, the stability of the job, the employment situation, and so on), but with such grandiosity as mentioned already. We get a view of Luke in therapy something like the following:

Therapist: These views of yourself . . . this imagery you have Luke
. . . what do you think about all of them?

    Patient: Oh I don't know, Doc, I just get carried away with a
new opportunity. I just go wild with the belief that I am a
world-beater.

Therapist: Do you think this fantasy, this imagery of yourself as a
champion of some sort has anything to do with your view of yourself? Or your *actual* success on the job?

    Patient: Yeah . . . I guess . . . maybe so . . . I really don't know.

Therapist: Do you think if you could start off with a better view
of yourself, more realistic imagery of yourself, you might fare better
on the actual job?

    Patient: I believe I might . . . but I am pretty stuck with this
tendency, you know.

Therapist: I know you are . . .

    Patient: (Interrupting) Yeah, I sure am.

Therapist: Can you tell me what actually happens in your thinking
when you land a new job . . . when you actually know you're hired?

    Patient: Well, I'm relieved that I *have* a job . . . you know. But
as soon as I know some of the details of the job, I guess I begin
to build up all this fantasy, and I see myself as a Walter Mitty
over and over.

Therapist: How often, or how much have any of these fantasies
paid off . . . come to realization?

    Patient: Oh . . . (laughs) . . . probably none! I guess I don't really
believe they will come true.

Therapist: But you believe in them somewhat . . . you fool yourself
for a while.

    Patient: Yeah, that's probably right . . . but I don't know just
where the matter breaks down.

Therapist: You have a strong tendency to construct the world as
you would like it to be—especially around the job situation—and you
don't yet know just how you slip into the pothole that seems to trip
you later.

The therapy with Luke took a while before it could make explicit
    the enormous reliance, unproductively, on grandiose fantasy and
    imagery. As time went by and Luke became more discerning of

how much he relied on imagery of the exaggerated and grandiose variety, he became more stable and was able to keep one job —as of the time therapy ended—over two years, a period of time much longer than he had ever been able to do before. His anxiety had been greatly reduced.

Luke's case is one of overly positive (but unrealistic) imagery. Others begin with more negative imagery and get into some "emotional hot water" via that route. A young woman, "Sarah," is a good example of such a tendency:

Patient: I am always afraid I or someone in my family is going to have a terrible accident . . . (crying) be maimed for life . . . or killed.

Therapist: This notion seems to plague you all the time?

Patient: It sure does (still crying). I just see one of my children . . . or my husband . . . or even a close friend lying there in the street, struck by a car . . . and perhaps dead or suffering . . .

Therapist: That's a pretty negative image you have of them and their life situation, isn't it?

Patient: Yes, it is . . . I just see them in all kinds of danger . . .

Therapist: I see . . . you are just in a constant state of anxiety and much of it comes from—or is supported by—a very negative image or view of yourself and your loved ones.

Patient: Yes, that seems . . . unfortunately . . . to be the case.

Therapist: I can well imagine that you are tense and anxious much of the time, especially when you have to deal with your loved ones leaving the house, riding in cars, doing all kinds of normal and common things . . .

Patient: (Interrupting) . . . That sounds bad to me but I must admit that it is true. I guess my thoughts are mostly negative.

Therapist: And with that you are in a stew all of the time . . . or much of the time?

Patient: And that is, unfortunately, true, too.

Therapist: You're anticipating danger all the time . . . and you are emotionally geared up for it in that you are tense and anxious to a corresponding degree?

Patient: I am, indeed, and I have been for some time now. That is the problem I want to work on . . . or at least it is part of the problem I *need* to work on.

Therapist: There are some things we can do to work on the problem. I might suggest that you note how and when you seem to conjure up these negative images of danger, destruction, foreboding events . . . and so on . . .

Patient: I just don't know now how and when they begin but I will try to find out.

Therapist: That is all that we can ask at this time . . . your effort and cooperation.

In the therapy with Sarah, we got into the negative imagery very quickly, once it had been designated as important in her anxiety, and proceeded to develop ways for her to identify the tendency very early in the process, and in time to foreshorten the tendency and eventually to largely preclude it. She started off thinking very negatively when she felt she was threatened in any way—and the threatening was not simply one of imagining physical danger and disaster, but other kinds of personal damage to her of a more psychological sort. She imagined the worst danger when she wasn't successful enough in persuading others to do as she, Sarah, wanted. In effect, Sarah was saying with her thoughts of dread and danger, and her accompanying anxiety, "If you don't do as I ask, or avoid doing what I want you to avoid, I am going to have an anxiety spell and imagine the worst . . . you stop this in me by doing as I ask you to do." This was an altogether unreasonable expectation on Sarah's part, but lacking the ability to actually discern what she was doing—how her negativism was related to her interpersonal behavior—she tended to keep on with it and the anxiety appeared to worsen over the months before she began therapy. The quickest attack on the anxiety and tension and related negative imagery was through making the imagery explicit and open and thereby subject to change—as long as the imagery was completely hidden, it was not open to change either by Sarah or through therapy.

IMAGERY AND RELAXATION

Imagery can help with relaxation training, too. You saw in the chapter on Relaxation (Chapter III) how important relaxation is as an antidote to tension and anxiety. One way the relaxation training proceeded was to use some imagery while exhaling (after taking a deep breath, for example) and to think as intensely and clearly as possible about the tension-provoking situation while exhaling. That's using imagery to assist the relaxation; it is also an excellent example of coupling the so-called "mental" aspects together with the bodily aspects, so that there is a total, frontal attack on the problem of anxiety. The more specifically the imagery can capture the tension and the anxiety, the better and more effective the relaxation procedure. You could not be asleep and do the relaxation (even if that were possible) and profit from it; you need to *concentrate* through the imagery, on the exact characteristics of the situation that produces the anxiety in real life. Even though the imagery is a substitute for the real thing, and constitutes a vicarious attack on the problem, it readies you for the real problem (the *in vivo* solution, itself), and it is good practice in helping to identify what it is in the real situation that is most tension producing.

WORDS CAN HELP TOO

Converting images into words is also important. Words move the imagery and what it stands for in the tension producing situation into reality, and words help us to deal with experiences, good or bad, tension-provoking or relaxing, more generally in our lives.

In this connection you can use words to capture the essence of the imagery associated with tension in several ways:

1. You can talk to yourself about the images that are identified as being related to anxiety and tension. "Oh, I see that it is the angry look on S's face that really upset me," you may say. It would be better to say it aloud, once identified, than to leave it at the imagery level. The imagery is a starter, a kind of beach head that often must be acknowledged and used first, but it yields, in time, to more overt consideration, because all efforts ultimately have to change behavior or they are not effective. When you are lying around passively, possibly grappling with a problem you have, speak aloud to yourself about the issue, state to yourself what the imagery includes. It will be helpful in dealing with the anxiety.

2. Confide in a close friend. Everyone has problems, and so talking about your own will not wreck a relationship if you allow the other person the same privilege. Say to the close friend, "You know I get this picture of ＿＿ again and again,

and everytime I do I get all upset. What do you think there is about me or this vision of _____ that can be so bothersome?" Bringing the subjective into the open is very healing, and often very reassuring.

3. If you like to paint or draw, or possibly construct a scene out of some art materials, you may try to objectify the images that bother you in these ways. Many times artists relieve personal tensions by such methods. You don't have to be an artist however to reveal your innermost thoughts, concerns, images, self-portraits and perhaps find some relief in this effort.

"Where is the *conflict* in imagery?" you may ask. If conflict is important, as we have said, in anxiety, where is the conflict in imagery?

All imagery, of course, is not related to anxiety. Since this is a book on anxiety management, we are of necessity concentrating only on imagery that is a problem, fraught with anxiety and tension. When the imagery is a product of anxiety, or tries to grapple with anxiety, there certainly is evidence of conflict.

Very often, the imagery you conjure up is, itself, an attempt to deal with conflict. You face a problem-situation, you think about it, you imagine certain things about the conflict (picturing yourself in some way), and the imagery is very frequently a representation to yourself of what the pros and cons are of the conflict. You see yourself now in one stance, now in another, in reference to what is troubling you. When you say you think things over and over, you also imagine them over and over again; you get into redundant or "vicious circle" routines and the images whirl along like a dervish just as thoughts do. The imagery that is an attempt to deal with conflict may also get caught up in the conflict, which is one reason for making the thoughts and images openly verbal (talking to yourself). Verbalizing the images and thoughts helps to bring them more into the open and to test out in real life what they mean.

IMAGERY AND WORRY

The relationship between imagery and worry has to be mentioned. If you examine your imagery closely, you may find that it is permeated with worry. The next time you notice yourself worrying, notice also if it is not related to images you are having about somebody, about yourself in relation to others, or perhaps it includes scenes in which some conflict has taken place. Worrying has to have some content, and the content is most likely to be images of interpersonal situations that are now, or have been, troubling to you.

This observation was brought to light in a therapeutic discussion with a patient we will call Charley:

Patient: I keep worrying about getting fired, you know—can't sleep, can't eat, not interested in anything. . .

Therapist: You have actually been warned about being fired by someone?

Patient: No, not really. I just fear it might happen.

Therapist: Does it seem to be related to anything that has happened on the job recently?

Patient: Well, some people have been fired, you know, but no one has said anything to me about it. But I just keep seeing my boss walking into my office one morning and saying, "Charley, we will not need your services after next Friday." This keeps going through my head, even in the daytime sometimes, but especially at night—I can't sleep and I roll and toss a lot.

Therapist: If there is a real chance you might be dismissed, that's one thing; if you are just worried on other grounds—some personal insecurity, for example—then we might attack the problem in that light.

Patient: Even if I don't get fired, and I hope I won't, I want to get over this worry, worry, worry, about it all the time.

Therapist: Let us begin with some examples of worrying about the problem—pick last night, or the night before for example . . . and let's deal with the worry very specifically.

It is not necessary to go into further detail in regard to Charley's therapy; suffice it to say he learned to attack the negative imagery of himself, the worry and fretting by verbalizing to his wife in the evening when and as the worry first started; and he made some notes on the content of his worry which he subsequently brought into the therapy hour. Many patients have problems besetting themselves similar to Charley's where there is a constant or recurrent scene depicting a real or imagined conflict; the scenario is played over and over without any new information being put into the system until some therapeutic intervention helps break the vicious circle of thought and worry.

Another way of helping to break the vicious circle of anxiety, whether it is accompanied by worry, negative imagery of one's self, or other features, is to set down in writing just what one experiences and try to institute some corrections based on this technique. The next chapter takes up this method.

WHAT IMAGERY have you engaged in during the past 24 hours that bears on the issues of anxiety in your life? See what you can do to bring these situations under better control.

Re: THE CONTROL OF IMAGERY
Things To Do

1. Think of a negative (anxiety-provoking) imagery or fantasy you've had in the past twenty-four to forty-eight hours. Talk out loud to yourself about it as if you were telling it to some one standing on your left. Then re-tell the imagery to someone standing on your right—still speaking aloud—and change the imagery (as you speak about it) to a positive outcome.

    e.g. "I have this image of myself as not being able to invite people in to a party and be a successful host. I see myself as 'all thumbs' and not knowing how to make others comfortable." (Said aloud to person on the left.)

    "Now I see people coming in to my house, I exchange pleasantries with them, invite them to help themselves to food and drink, and I make an effort to speak at least briefly with each one during the evening."

ADDITIONAL READINGS

How To Make It With Another Person by Richard B. Austin, McMillan, New York, 1976.

The Courage To Create, by Rollo May, Norton Publ., New York, 1975.

Scripts People Live: Transactional Analysis of Life Scripts by Claude M. Steiner, Grove Press, New York, 1975.

Power! How To Get It, How To Use It by Michael Korda, Random House, New York, 1975.

The Fantasy Game—How Male and Female Fantasies Affect Our Lives by Peter Dally, Dell Press, New York, 1975.

Beginning Without End by Sam Keen, Harper & Row, New York, 1975.

With Heart and Mind by Richard Taylor, St. Martin's Press, 1973.

Chapter V

Reducing anxiety
by writing

The various methods of reducing anxiety discussed in earlier chapters —assertiveness, relaxation, and noting how much negative imagery one may harbor—can be enlarged upon by a discussion of the use of writing.

People seldom note how powerful and useful for changing behavior writing down things may be—for purposes of memory, for purposes of making communications with others clearer and more reliable, and now for purposes of controlling and reducing anxiety. We use writing in many kinds of legal and formal communications with others—signing checks, contracts, writing letters, and so forth, so why not use writing to assist ourselves in overcoming anxiety?

Several factors make writing an attractive technique for handling anxiety:

1. It is easily available. One need carry only a pen or pencil and a note pad.
2. Writing can be engaged in on-the-spot, that is, when and where the anxiety occurs.
3. Writing makes the underlying issues concrete and more easily discernible.

4. By writing down your concerns, you are forced to do more than just fret about them, you have to *do* something that distracts you momentarily and opens up new ways of behaving in regard to the anxiety.

5. You *admit* to yourself that the anxiety is perplexing and uncomfortable, then move on toward solutions.

6. Part of the writing can be directed toward a real solution; that is, what you can do is specified in the writing.

7. Writing does not solve the whole anxiety problem, but it is a useful "stop-gap" measure that can serve well until more long-range solutions are found (improved assertiveness, for example).

8. Writing provides a record. Keep your notebook of "writings" so that you can see, over time, how you have handled previous problems, and this can assist you in meeting new ones. Writing shows your progress over time!

AN EXAMPLE OF WRITING

Several examples of using writing will illustrate further the above points.

One patient, called Jane, came in for therapy owing to "anxiety spells" she was having on the job. She reported she would worry (there's the worry and imagery again!) about her conversation with her roommate the evening before whenever they had one of their frequent misunderstandings. These worry sessions on the job were very distracting to her and reduced her activity there to only very routine matters; sometimes, even, she would leave work and go home crying over her distress. Some excerpts from Jane's talk with her therapist bring the issue to life:

Patient: I just have the worst problems working when I get into one of my spells.

Therapist: **What actually happens during one of these spells?**

Patient: Well, I get to thinking about my conversation—or I should say argument with Paula, she's my roommate—and I just carry it on and on in my job. I called her up once when it was bad and talking with her did no good . . . in fact, it made me feel worse.

Therapist: **You've considered other living arrangements?**

Patient: Yes, but they are not feasible.

Therapist: And you feel you've tried to get the issues settled amicably with your roommate, Paula?

Patient: Yes, but to no avail, so far, anyhow.

Therapist: One problem we now face, if I understand you correctly, is that all this problem with your roommate disables you on the job?

Patient: Very much so . . .

Therapist: So we could say we have this issue about the job as an *immediate* one, while working out problems with Paula, your roommate, is important but not as immediate in one sense.

Patient: I guess you could say that . . . but the problems with Paula are still pretty important, even with job aside.

Therapist: Quite so!

Patient: But you have a point—I am most concerned right now with not being able to perform on the job.

Therapist: O.K., let's get down to brass tacks about the job situation —tell me precisely how it goes there for you.

Patient: I usually do all right in the morning because I am the busiest then, with the mail and everything.

Therapist: But in the afternoon . . .?

Patient: That's when I have the worst time.

Therapist: And . . .

Patient: Well, I usually talk with Paula during the noon hour—she calls me or I call her . . . and that can often end up in a spat about a lot of things . . . buying groceries, cleaning the apartment, having in guests . . . and I guess just about everything.

Therapist: Then, after the phone call to Paula . . .?

Patient: I just worry and fume over our talk.

Therapist: What if you didn't talk with her during the noon hour, as one way of minimizing the anxiety?

Patient: I have thought about that and we have agreed to speak less often over the phone, but I still worry over the evening before, or the next evening.

Therapist: Maybe an agreement in the evening, or even in the morning to not talk during the day, but pick up the issues when you are face to face again would be desirable?

Patient: I can talk with Paula about that. (Pause) You see, I really like her and I don't want to move—and she doesn't either —and I always feel we can work it out . . . but we never do, and this bugs me the next day, or for several days.

Therapist: Understandably! That is, given the conditions you describe.

Patient: But if we don't talk at noon, will I feel *that* much better on the job?

Therapist: That remains to be seen . . . I don't know . . . and you will need to be the judge, ultimately.

Patient: Well, anything is worth trying right now . . . I really feel terrible.

Therapist: And we can try a writing technique, so called, on the job that may help to control anxiety.

Patient: How's that?

Therapist: Well, when you feel you are getting upset, simply write down something like the following: "Although I am angry and upset with Paula, I will not let that distract me from my work—I will admit I am concerned but put it aside for now and go back to my work."

Patient: Sounds superficial . . . how can I do that?

Therapist: In a way it is superficial, but superficial things can often work well momentarily.

Patient: Yes, that's true enough. (Pause) You say I just write down something . . .?

Therapist: You don't write down "just something," but specifically how you feel and what you are confronted with—# 1, you are upset—

Patient: (Interrupting) True enough—I got that . . .

Therapist: All right, #1, you are upset; #2, you admit to yourself that is true—you don't try to set it aside or say to yourself, "I shouldn't let that worry me . . ." which really doesn't help; #3, writing it down requires concentration on *that* task; #4, you end by saying you put aside the concern and then get back to work. It frees you up for the work at hand *after* admitting openly you have the problem but cannot do anything long range *at that time.*

Patient: I see—well, it makes sense that way.

Therapist: All we can ask is that you give it a fair try. (Pause) You may need to use it several times.

Patient: Oh, I see.

Therapist: After all, you've built up a load of anxiety and anger, and it won't dissipate very fast you know.

Patient: Probably not . . . I see (Pause) . . . I see.

Therapist: Let's give it a concrete try right now . . . Imagine yourself in the situation at work, you've just had an unsatisfactory phone conversation with Paula, following an unresolved problem this morning, or last night, and you are ready to write about it in the manner I suggested, using your own words.

Patient: All right. (Patient begins to write on end of desk, talking aloud to herself as she writes . . .) O.K., here's what I have written: "I don't want to argue with Paula . . . I want matters resolved . . . and I want to get back to work."

Therapist: That may be all right if it serves you satisfactorily, but it is not quite the *whole* idea. (Pause) The idea includes admitting *first* that you are anxious—you started out by saying you didn't want to argue with Paula, but you *are* arguing with Paula . . . so let's begin with the facts . . .

Patient: I see. (Pause) I should say something like . . . "Although I am upset with Paula . . ." and then go on with the rest. "Although I am upset . . . dum-dee-dum-dee . . ."

Therapist: Exactly. You see, you must concretely admit where you are *at*—at the time. You *are* upset . . . angry . . . begin with that fact. No dum-dee-dum to it!

Patient: Yes, that is the most important thing, isn't it? I must begin by admitting I am upset. Right now, I'm not, and so I may be a bit superficial—you must know.

Therapist: I do believe you are treating it more lightly than would be the case when you are actually caught up in your anxiety.

Patient: O.K., now I am resolved to whip this problem. I write down what I said, and end by saying, "I will not let this distract me . . . I will get back to work."

Therapist: Very well for the time being. Let's see how it goes between now and next time.

Jane, our patient, began to settle down a bit during the next three days before the next session. She was a bit facetious and glib during this session with her therapist, saying that a problem not present at the time cannot be too serious, even though she had spoken of considerable distress a bit earlier in the same session. The next session began to produce some results in that she was upset by her roommate, Paula, and she—Jane—did begin writing down her feelings on the job. Here is her report a few days later:

Patient: Well, I realize I was a bit silly here last time, because Paula and I did get into it some and it disturbed me considerably on the job. I tried the writing—I tried it several times before I actually *did* it.

Therapist: I don't understand . . .

Patient: I mean I got out my pencil—well, I already had the pencil on my desk—I got ready to write and then quit.

Therapist: Didn't write at all?

Patient: That's right—I didn't write the first time or two because I wasn't sure . . . I guess I just didn't have confidence . . . and then I figured, well, I am trying to do this and so I might as well get down to it.

Therapist: Maybe you have some problems being serious about matters unless they are pressing on you right then.

Patient: Out of sight—out of mind?

Therapist: Perhaps.

In a subsequent meeting, the issues became more clear cut with Jane and between herself and her roommate, Paula. Jane buckled down and began to be more serious about her plight and about doing the writing as a way of coping with her anxiety. Her more earnest effort is reflected in the following conversation:

Patient: Well, I got down to business this week and did it.

Therapist: And what, exactly, did you do?

Patient: I did the writing when I was upset . . . anxious . . . angry . . . and all that. And it *did* help. I was surprised!

Therapist: You feel you gave it a good test and it proved useful to you?

Patient: I sure do.

Therapist: Tell me, now, what you did and when and how . . .

Patient: Well, last Monday (today is Thursday, isn't it?—Yes) . . . well last Monday morning, Paula and I had a big fight . . . a really big one, the biggest we've ever had . . . and when I got to work, I could hardly contain myself. I could hardly hold my cup of coffee about 9:30, I was still so jittery . . . so I said to myself,

"This nonsense has got to stop—I'm going to write all this down, like he said," and so I did! I wrote ..."I ..." that's how I started, then I changed it ... "Although I am upset with the argument with Paula and hate her guts, I will not let her pull me down this way ... I will not be distracted by her nonsense —I'm going to do my work!" And by golly I did! I really turned her off. I really washed her out of my hair!

Therapist: Just like that?

Patient: Well, maybe not that fast ... but I got rid of her annoying me by writing it several times—is that O.K.?

Therapist: It is all right ... you use it as you see fit—it is only a tool and not a commitment.

This relatively long excerpt from Jane's case was cited in order to bring out several points in regard to using writing in the face of anxiety, anger, and upset. First, Jane had to be shown the seriousness of using writing. Because she took the method so lightly, she rejected it several times. Sometimes people react this way. They just cannot see that such a simple thing can be effective. Second, she had to be pushed further into the use of writing because of her increased tensions. She had to be pushed to the brink before she would give writing a chance, since she had no other clear alternative but to stew in her own emotional juice. Third, when she finally used the writing enough to see it could help her, she took it over as a more or less standard technique to use during her kind of anxiety clutch. She later reported that she used the writing when she had a series of misunderstandings with her mother, a person who in the past had really put her down terribly, she reported, and by whom she had been emotionally devastated.

Writing may be used not only in the limited "first aid" sense discussed above, but may actually constitute the main thrust of therapy and carry the main load of therapy. That is, the whole of therapy may be carried on by writing without any oral, face to face interviews at all. Writing has been shown in such a context to help shorten the totality of therapy, to make each writing session shorter and thereby more effective than a full hour of interviewing, and to increase the clarity of communication between patient and therapist. It is likely that writing will be used to a greater extent as both a major mode of therapy and as an adjunct to therapy in the manner discussed in this chapter.

WRITING AN AGENDA FOR YOURSELF

Writing may be used not only in the anxiety clutches you experience, but also as an agenda-setting device. We all make notes for grocery lists, telephone numbers and the like; we can use writing to assist us in preventing or reducing anxiety situations. Several points along this line include the following:

1. Make an overall schedule of your time and activities, starting with when you arise in the morning and ending with actual bedtime. Put in travel time, time for shopping, even wasted time. Account for the entirety of your activities. All this goes in one column.
2. In the second column, put in the actual times you spent in these activities—compare your *budgeted time* with your actual *expenditure* of time.
3. After budgeting your effort in this way for a week or two, revise the schedule and make it fit more closely between the "ideal" and the "actual" expenditures of time.

Try to stay as close to the budgeted time and effort as you can, moving toward a natural acceptance of the schedule to the point where you need not even think about it. Sometimes people object to schedules as being "too rigid" but actually we all live on schedules—our bodies live on schedules, and life depends upon them to a great extent—whether we recognize it or not. Using writing here to schedule time and effort is simply a matter of capitalizing on a procedure you use in rough form anyhow; this way, you can firm it up, take out the kinks, and find yourself working on a new and more natural schedule without any strain. If you find you have trouble with such an undertaking, sit down and write out the "pros" and "cons" of what you are trying to do and see if that doesn't iron out the difficulty: "Although I do not like making a formal schedule, I am going to try it to see how it works for me." "Even though it seems rigid, I know a schedule will help me with my time and effort and keep me from getting into anxiety-provoking time-binds." And so forth...

A little different tactic is taken in the next chapter—a matter of judicious and tactical use of situations to overcome anxiety where the approach is more indirect and very flexible.

THINK about what you have read
in this chapter, jot down the
main points, and list some
ways you can benefit yourself
thereby.

Re: THE USE OF WRITING

Things To Do

1. Write down in advance whenever you feel you will have a confrontation with someone producing anxiety.

   e.g. "I have to meet Bill for lunch and he always makes me anxious." or "I'll accept his making me anxious and I'll try to talk about neutral subjects."

2. Similarly, write down after-the-fact anxiety provocations.

   e.g. "I was upset by Wendy at the dinner party when she made a slighting remark about my dress but I wrote it down and then avoided her briefly until I felt I could talk to her about our car-pooling the kids next week."

3. Keep a weekly record of all writing efforts and what they were about. Name the person and the event.

	Sun.	Mon.	Tues.	Wed.	Thurs.	Fri.	Sat.
1		Mable/dress		Mable/ picnic		grocer return fd.	
2	church/ choir		Tom/ fix tire				church/ clean-up
3				Sam,Steve house wk.			
4	church/ sing-choir						

ADDITIONAL READINGS

Short-Term Psychotherapy and Structural Behavior Change by E. Lakin Phillips and Daniel N. Wiener, Prentice-Hall, New Jersey, 1966.

Creative Coping: A Guide To Positive Living by Julius Fast, Morrow, New Jersey, 1976.

The Relaxation Response by Herbert Bereson with Marian Klipper, Morrow, New York, 1975.

Chapter VI

Staying away (temporarily) from anxiety-provoking situations

Sometimes people think that if they dodge an anxiety provoking situation they are "copping out" and that is injurious to them. However, a *strategic* or *tactical* avoidance of anxiety is not copping out; it may actually be the opposite.

Also, since anxiety is *recurrent*, there is always another chance to cope with it. Avoidance of anxiety is one situation and on occasion will not damage one's problem-solving ability. It may even enhance it if some of the recommendations given below are followed.

There are several ways in which anxiety is recurrent:

1. Situations where anxiety is forced upon you.
2. Anxiety situations you stumble into.
3. Anxiety situations you have to handle gradually, or over time.
4. Anxiety situations as part of growth and development.

We may take these up one at a time.

Situations where anxiety is forced upon you are more common than you may think. Some examples may include:

A. Being called upon regularly to recite in a classroom.
B. Taking examinations.

    C. Serving on committees and making reports.

    D. Getting disturbing news about yourself, family members or friends.

    E. Being interviewed for some job or job promotion.

    F. Being called into "court" for some offense you allegedly committed.

    G. Being attacked or accused—in traffic, in a store, on the street—by someone who is taking his/her aggression out on you.

    H. Participating in conflict between groups, one of which you belong to—e.g., neighborhood groups, one of which favors a given action (say, licensing all the dogs and cats in the area) and the other opposing this action.

And there may well be other examples which you can think of.

You can get your attitude ready for these kinds of situations where tension and anxiety are put on you: firstly, by *anticipating* them; secondly, by *rehearsing* for them; thirdly, by *acknowledging* that they will occur and not easily go away; and fourthly, by *discerning* that these situations, although distasteful and unwanted, will not devastate you.

You may cope *longer range* with these tension-arousing situations by doing one or more of the things discussed thus far in this book: by relaxation, by assertiveness, by catching a hold of your imagery and worry and bringing them under control, and by using writing techniques to assist. However, the immediate short-run is also important.

ANXIETY SITUATIONS THRUST UPON YOU

Having tension and anxiety thrust upon you will occur as long as you live, there is no magic way to discard them; there are only available the best ways to cope with them. The longer the lead time you have before the anxiety provoking situation occurs, the better; and the more resourceful you are, in terms of employing the techniques discussed herein, the sooner you can possibly prevent control and override the anxiety. Some examples of useful anticipatory procedures in handling anxiety and tension can be reviewed in the case of "Debbie":

Debbie complained in her therapy that she could not deal with phone calls from friends and acquaintances calling her to serve on religious committees, to help with day-care programs, or to serve on community groups to deal with a local park and its problems. She was active in all these larger organizations—church, welfare, community—but preferred not to be assigned a particular role or be called to serve in some specific capacity. When she could volunteer on her own, which she seldom did, she was more comfortable, but the fact that others solicited her time, effort and interest bothered her. As she said, "Because I express my views at meetings that committees never have enough active members, I get many calls." She became distressed with calls to serve and was unable to handle them without considerable anxiety. She knew the calls would come to her but had to learn to be better prepared. The therapy was concerned with this problem, since she was not going to entirely absent herself from all social interest.

Patient: I got two more of those damn calls last night and I just couldn't sleep all night—they really upset me.

Therapist: **You went to the meeting on the use of the park and so now you're being solicited for help.**

Patient: Yes, that's correct. I was *there* and I am interested, but I don't want to work on a committee.

Therapist: **Is there another role you would or could play?**

Patient: Well . . . maybe . . . maybe I could volunteer for some specific job, but I don't want to serve with others on a committee and have all the bother about meetings and where and when and who will do what job and all that junk.

Therapist: **I see. It is not so much the work that you are wanting to avoid as it is the committee and organizational aspects themselves.**

Patient: Yeah, that's right. I want to go straight to a job and do it and not have all this fooling around that only makes me impatient and nervous . . . (pause) . . . and so when I get a phone call to do something, I think of all the junk that goes with it and I just get mad.

Therapist: **Maybe that's a big part of your anxiety—anger! (Pause) You're angry because you don't want them to bother you, yet your experience shows that this thing comes up several times a month and will continue to do so as long as you show your face at these meetings.**

Patient: I guess so—it's a problem that keeps coming up and I am getting worn out by it.

Therapist: What do you actually say when you are called—give me chapter and verse . . .

Patient: Well, I talk with the person and I try to be nice and show interest and all that . . .

Therapist: And so such a person needing a committee member reads you as available and interested—is that unusual?

Patient: No, I guess not, but I say I am not available.

Therapist: You mean you say with *some* words that you are not available, but with *other* words and actions you are.

Patient: Well, just being nice and pleasant doesn't mean you *are* available.

Therapist: Perhaps not, but it can certainly be read that way—people are going ahead on what you say, on how you sound, on the fact that you were at the meeting, that you are now talking on the phone about related problems. You end up turning them down, but before that you are angry. This prevents sleep and causes anxiety.

Patient: You are saying that perhaps I am not taking a straight line with them?

Therapist: That seems to me to be true.

Patient: So what do I need to do to straighten it all out?

Therapist: What do you think?

Patient: I don't know—I thought I was doing it right.

Therapist: Then why are you so anxious? Something is wrong.

Patient: Yes . . . you're right . . . you're right . . . I never quite saw it that way. (Pause) You have a point there.

Therapist: Yes, very likely. (Pause) You have some ideas as to how to cope?

Patient: I could tell them at the outset that I do not want to serve on a *committee.*

Therapist: That would doubtlessly be a good starter.

Patient: Or I could volunteer for a given job at the general meeting, if I could find such a job—I don't know, maybe I couldn't.

Therapist: That's an alternative also. Sounds like you've thought of a couple of constructive things.

Patient: I will keep getting the calls—(sighs)—I guess as long as I live—or live *here* anyhow.

Therapist: Yes, you are in the mainstream of activity.

Patient: I could just go to the meetings—there's one tomorrow night about some school problems and day-care—and pick and choose, or decide not to pick or choose anything, and try to handle it that way.

Therapist: Then if you're called for a job, what then?

Patient: I'll say I already have a job . . . and . . .

Therapist: And?

Patient: And just not talk so much or so long about it—say I have a job—just cut it off then and there.

Therapist: That would be asserting yourself.

Patient: I'm beginning to see what we're talking about here. I just have to pick something—if I want to do something—and let it go at that. I keep getting calls because I do not act decisively.

Therapist: You seem to have a pretty good verbal grasp of the matter —now let's see what you *actually* do about it.

Debbie made some progress in the next two or three weeks in *anticipating* calls from others to get her to serve on committees and she stopped assuming she would not have to explain her situation to them. She stopped assuming that "being nice" would always lead the other person to see what she, Debbie, was trying to accomplish. The dual and conflictive message—interest vs. no interest (or no willingness to work on committees)—was a garbled message that Debbie gave; and she gave it over and over, all to her own anxiety risk, without realizing that she should know in advance that she would have the same problem to meet over and over if she did not change her outlook.

STUMBLING INTO ANXIETY SITUATIONS

There are many anxiety situations you stumble into as well. Some of them include:

    A. Having to introduce people you hardly know to others you hardly know (or maybe you know them and can't remember the names), all to your embarrassment.

    B. Making decisions on the spot where there is little or no

time to get information, mull it over, or follow up on the consequences of your action.

C. Facing people you meet accidentally on the street, in church, or in the marketplace, where you are embarrassed about your previous behavior.

It is difficult if not impossible to prepare for an emergency, except in a general sense. You can have candles available if your electric power goes off; or a spare can of gasoline in case your car runs dry. But it is hard to have a specific remedy to an anxiety situation that you just accidentally run into, unless the accidental part can really be played down and you prepare for any exigency. You might realize that sooner or later you will run into that former neighbor you used to know, and with whom you had the fight over the property line; so you could have in mind some anxiety-reducing tactics in the event the neighbor is found to be in line just ahead of you at a movie or facing you across the table in a randomly assigned seat at a church banquet.

Each of these kinds of situations calls for some fast foot work. You can excuse yourself from the situation and try to think of something to say or do while you are momentarily away; you can speak to the person or persons, ask for a reminder of names (if your memory is lacking), or otherwise update your information; or you can try to ignore the whole matter. The latter may not work very well because it is more a total avoidance than it is a matter of temporary side-stepping, and it may complicate the situation because it contains no real problem-solving. Just as Debbie in our example above had to realize that chronic problems *do* reoccur, you have to realize equally well that even random problems will likely reoccur; you should therefore be generally ready for them.

Readiness takes the form of being realistic about situations you may face. If there is some likelihood you will be embarrassed to see a former friend, foe or adversary at church or elsewhere, think about what you may say or do, especially if the meeting is face-to-face. What is most realistic in such a case? To speak briefly, then move on? To smile and nod and say nothing? To look angry and scowl? To try to strike up a conversation about some neutral topic, or about some topic you know either of them is concerned with? Generally the more assertive you can be, the better; as this gives you confidence that you are doing something constructive, and that you have, so to speak, the upper hand. You are therefore less likely to be put down by the interaction. Later, of course, if your anxiety has not been well managed and you still carry a load of tension, so to speak, you will need to use one or more of the methods already described in earlier chapters: Relaxation, assertiveness, imagery examination, writing down the concern.

GRADUAL HANDLING OF ANXIETY

Some anxiety situations are those you cannot meet all at once; you have to handle them gradually. An example would be that of taking a course in public speaking where for several weeks you have to give either a prepared or impromptu speech of a few minutes at each session of the class. Likewise if you are a singer or actor in local choral or theatre groups and find yourself anxious when you have to perform on several occasions. These types of situations, often arranged to be of benefit to the anxious person, can really help you overcome tension since the opportunity to readjust to the anxiety is available again and again. You can, in such circumstances, give part of a speech, stop, get criticism, relax, and then resume the speech, or, you can give the whole speech, get comments, and then give it again, always moving toward greater and greater confidence and relaxation. Sometimes, giving the same speech, or acting the same part several times, can reduce the anxiety down to near-zero and raise your confidence at the same time.

Lacking a formal setting in which to work out the anxiety connected with speaking, musical performing or acting, you can still run through these roles openly in your own home, have family members listen or watch—and criticize constructively—and then redo them several times, again relaxing with each performance and bringing the anxiety down to zero. The more times you can disperse anxiety in these kinds of controlled situations, the more likely you are to find the real performance a matter of comfort and personal confidence.

Any complicated role that is associated with acting, musicianship, or speaking, will take a number of sessions to bring on the desired results, and the whole undertaking should be viewed as a kind of course, not alone a matter of handling an episode (important as that is on occasion).

YOUR "ANXIETY-PRONE" QUOTIENT

Since all people experience anxiety in some amount on some occasions, you should know *your* own tendencies in this regard.
You might call this your "A-P Quotient," or "Anxiety-Prone
Quotient." This quotient business is not meant to be emphasized,
nor is it intended to make you think of yourself as permanently
anxiety-ridden; but simply to help you represent as realistically
as you can this particular amount of self-knowledge. Anyone
can be made anxious just as anyone can become physically ill;
to recognize this kind of vulnerability is only a matter of admitting that we are all human. However, you do not want to
succumb to the notion, or carry around in your head—so to
speak—a feeling that you are just about to run into some anxiety
provoking situation so you'd better be extra careful. Such living
on tenterhooks is, itself, a manifestation of anxiety, and certainly
something—in the spirit of this book—to be overcome or avoided.

If you think about your "Anxiety-Prone Quotient" just enough to
identify some realistic areas that bother you, then the "A-P
Quotient" idea is worthwhile. If the "A-P Quotient" idea bothers
you very much, then you are probably not facing up to some
self-knowledge that may be important. Look at the following
brief list of Anxiety-Prone situations that have been noticed
and reported by many people, and compare yourself with the
total list; mark the ones that apply to you:

1. I think something dreadful may happen to me.
2. I have friends and acquaintances I hate to meet on the
   street (or in stores).
3. I am bothered by thoughts that keep me unhappy (or
   prevent sleep).
4. I am embarrassed about promises I have made to people
   that I have not kept.
5. I hate to ask someone for a favor.
6. I hate to admit openly that I have strong feelings about
   some things.
7. I get angry when I express an opinion, so I just keep still
   when the topic comes up.
8. I feel I am less able to cope with life than I was a few
   years ago.
9. The things that bother me most, I just put out of my mind.
10. Some kinds of people really disturb me.

11. I am always afraid that most people don't like me.
12. When I am talking with someone, I keep thinking about other things.
13. A lot of people aren't friendly toward me.
14. I feel I have to be jovial and pleasant all the time.
15. I find I dislike too many things.
16. A lot of my friends are very critical toward me.
17. I often drum my fingers on a chair or desk.
18. I have more nervous habits than I like to admit.
19. I am always worrying about something.
20. I never seem to get things done.
21. I worry about what my friends say to me.
22. I keep mulling over things I have said or done in the past.
23. Everyone seems to have little mannerisms that annoy me.
24. I often don't feel like "being nice to people."
25. Most people don't care how I feel.

The list could, of course, be greatly expanded. There are formal tests available which survey very systematically the general problem of personal anxiety; you can get "readings" on these tests from a licensed or certified psychologist.

It is equally important to emphasize that any anxiety (almost) can be overcome. You just have to work judiciously and intelligently at the task. However, there are some anxieties that probably cannot be fully overcome; and you think here of anxiety associated with death of a loved one, prolonged illness of your own or of a loved one; the disastrous results of an accident that leave a person maimed for life; and the like. The persistent nature of some of life's unfortunate events and consequences can leave you anxious enough to say that anxiety pretty well dominates your life. However, in recent years, even these seemingly intractible anxieties are being whittled down to size—therapy is helping people who have terminal illnesses, probably the most anxiety-provoking situation any one can face. And new methods of treatment—many of them employing our familiar assertive, relaxative and related measures—are gradually cutting anxiety down to a more manageable size.

The more we learn about anxiety management by following procedures addressed here, the sooner we will be able to bring ever more control into this problem area for our own benefit and comfort. Anxiety-prone situations are neither so certain that we all must succumb, nor are they so easy to handle that we can afford to take them lightly; they are as ubiquitous as the common cold and, like the cold, can be passing or formidable.

Anxiety avoidance as opposed to copping out, might be thought of in terms of some common social situations that call for solution. Some of them are illuminated below.

1. When you are concerned about your health and/or about personal comfort when among others who smoke (especially among others who chain smoke), you can be made very anxious by this kind of confrontation. Should you ask others not to smoke at all in your presence? Should the "no smoking" be confined to dining at a table where people are in close proximity and the personal discomfort from tobacco smoke is particularly great? Should you confine your "no smoking" attitude only to your own home (or car), and give up on the matter in other settings? More and more you see signs in taxis, in elevators, in restaurants, in buses and airplanes, that prohibit smoking. This kind of public support frees you as a non-smoker to state your case to others, and reduces your anxiousness in coping with smoking in social settings. A moderately assertive role might be taken by the non-smoker who is made uncomfortable and also anxious by those smoking in his/her presence: "I prefer that you not smoke at the table." "Smokers may go into that room and the non-smokers may remain in here." "This room is so close, I think smoking should take place outside—don't you agree?" And so forth . . .

In a way, protesting the smoking of others clashes with the privileges provided the smoker—has he not a right to smoke if he so chooses? This conflict ends in making the non-smoker under-assertive and therefore anxious when meeting the problem. Although people are bound to differ on this issue, the matter must be understood as not one of taking the stand than another person cannot smoke at all, but rather that smoking is best confined to situations where others are not offended. Certainly most of our social graces follow such a plan, and there is no reason not to try to bring the control of smoking under such aegis. A gentle and fair amount of control will reduce everyone's anxiety since smokers often smoke because they are socially anxious; and may be made even more anxious—and not know what else to do—when they know others protest their smoking.

2. A similar occasion for anxiety in the short-haul may be noted when the owner-driver of a car requests that others wear seat belts when riding in the owner's car. These are assertive rights that reduce anxiety for the owner-driver, if such a person does not try to be a "nice guy," say nothing, and bottle up his conflictive anxiety. The law in most principalities, as well as readily available car safety measures, supports the use of seat belts; this can offer a measure of comfort to the person who is anxious about enforcing safety practices on his car occupants. To follow sensible safety rules here can move social interchange in the direction of easy communication that prevents anxiety.

A general rule to follow in all of these types of anxiety-provoking situations is to ask yourself what you prefer to have happen, what would allow you the most personal comfort, and what would appear to be the best and most comfortable practice for others. If you can bring these two sets of interest together, then you have advanced yourself along the road toward avoiding anxieties, and also developed a means of reducing anxieties in social situations that are largely due to the behavior of others.

LIST SOME anxiety-provoking situations you are likely to encounter and decide whether you want to avoid them temporarily and encounter them directly. Jot down this decision.

Re: AVOIDING ANXIETY SITUATIONS
Things To Do

1. Write down all the *anxiety provoking situations* you experienced in the last
    week and what you might have done to avoid (or recognize) them.

    e.g.

wk.	Sun.	Mon.	Tues.	Wed.	Thurs.	Fri.	Sat.
1st	talked on phone excuse self						
2nd		got bad tomatoes returned for refund		didn't re-turn embar-rassing call later on returned			
3rd			passed up receiving line went back 5 min. later	.		avoided telling hus-band re: bills brought up later	
4th							anx. about calling re: car-pool called later after rehearsing

2. Think of up-coming anxiety situations you can (possibly) temporarily avoid
    if you are very anxious and don't let yourself off the hook—do the anxiety
    thing as soon as possible.

    e.g. Call and say you can't cashier at the school fund-raising and book sale.
    Practice the call on the phone as a "dummy" call first, then dial all but
    the last digit and give your message, then go through with the whole
    thing.

ADDITIONAL READINGS

Own Your Own Life by Richard G. Abell with Cloris W. Abell, David McKay, New York, 1976.

The You That Could Be by Fitzhugh Dodson, Follett, Chicago, 1976.

Discipline, Achievement and Mental Health, 2nd edition, by E. Lakin Phillips and Daniel N. Wiener, Prentice-Hall, New Jersey, 1972.

Chapter VII

Attacking and Mastering anxiety-provoking situations

This whole book has been devoted to the management of anxiety. In this chapter the issue taken up will be that of directly *attacking anxiety* when and where it occurs. This direct effort is not to be construed as opposite or contradictory to that of the theme in the last chapter—temporarily avoiding or staying away from anxiety-provoking situations in order to get a new lease on the problem—but as an alternative. You need all the resourcefulness you can muster in handling anxiety; and there is nothing wrong with the proposition that at one time you may attack the anxiety directly while at another time you may temporarily side step it for tactical or strategic purposes.

Some anxiety situations you must attack (or approach, if attack is too strong a word for you) directly in order to prove to yourself that you can do the job! Some anxiety situations may not allow for indirect or side-stepping measures and you have to come up with the direct approach or else forfeit opportunity altogether for the time being. One person facing this kind of problem was Margaret, a young adult looking for a job in an advertising agency, who evidenced much anxiety when approaching the interview time with a prospective employer or when making calls to agencies in order to set up an interview. Margaret tells her story:

Patient: I've been out of school six months now and I don't have a job jet.

Therapist: But you've been pounding the pavement?

Patient: Well . . . yes and no. I go at it now and then but the trouble is that I get so anxious about applying for a job I just about die . . . (pause) . . . I get scared too easily and I don't follow through.

Therapist: And it is pretty important that you follow them?

Patient: Certainly. (Pause) Just yesterday I was supposed to go for an interview at 1:30 in the afternoon at an agency. I couldn't eat lunch, but I forced myself to eat something and then I got so upset I vomited and turned so white I would have been a disaster to see.

Therapist: You bugged out then?

Patient: Yes, I did . . . (pause) . . . and I am so humiliated I cannot stand it—I'm even ashamed to tell you . . . and I couldn't talk later with my mother on the phone about how I did.

Therapist: Can you tell me specifically what you do when you are confronted with such anxiety attacks?

Patient: Well, . . . I try to talk to myself and tell myself it is not a life and death matter and that I shouldn't be so upset and that everything will turn out all right—you know, the usual stuff.* (Pause) What do you think?

Therapist: Well, I am thinking of several things—possibly both direct and indirect attacks or approaches to your anxiety spells, if we can call them that.

Patient: I am desperate enough to try or do anything.

Therapist: The direct approach to the anxiety is not to give in but to keep the appointment—in the instance you cited—and go through with it anyway.

Patient: But I feel like I can't . . .

---

*The reader will recognize immediately the relevance of the Writing chapter for this young girl's problem—she begins, not by admitting the problem, but by trying to gainsay it, a technique almost bound to fail.

Therapist: I know you do but with a little bit of judicious help I am sure you can.

Patient: And what might that be?

Therapist: I started to say there is a direct approach and an indirect one . . . we should use both.

Patient: O.K. What are each of these?

Therapist: First off, don't let yourself avoid the interview—go through with it anyhow. You will see as you get into it that you *can* manage.

Patient: Well, maybe.

Therapist: You can challenge all I say when and as you employ the techniques, but for now just try to understand and put into operation what I suggest.

Patient: All right, I'll quit raising objection then.

Therapist: The direct attack includes several things—go to the place of the interview *several times* before the actual day and hour of the interview, make your tracks, so to speak, get used to going there, talk to yourself at the time about anxiety.

Patient: That doesn't sound too hard to do.

Therapist: And . . . as you make these trips to the interview place —and here comes the second or indirect approach—say to yourself, "I know I am anxious . . . I am scared to death . . . I wish I didn't have to do this . . . I am all mixed up but I need the job . . ." Any words or sentences that *capture* in words how you feel.

Patient: I see . . . admit I am upset.

Therapist: Exactly. (Pause) *But,* don't let the admitting drive you off; don't run away. If you have to, go one-half the way from your home to the interview site; then stop and talk to yourself; then go on a distance; then stop and talk again; keep this up until you get there.

Patient: Instead of doing what I did which was to bug out.

Therapist: Yes, that's the idea. Don't break and run. Keep the direct momentum going; stay in there; play the game. But, help yourself with the tension and anxiety of the moment *by admitting you are upset* and you will not let this drive you off. A little formula might go like this: "Although I am anxious as I can be and scared to death, I am not going to stop . . . I am going through with the interview." And you will see that it will very likely help you—it won't kill off all the anxiety but it will reduce it.

Patient: I see. (Pause) In a way I was doing *two* things wrong?

Therapist: Yes . . . what do you mean?

Patient: I was first being driven off by the anxiety . . . and *that* is incorrect . . . (pause), and . . . and . . . I was trying to make the anxiety go away by not admitting how real and important it was.

Therapist: That's a very good way to put the issues . . . you were doing two wrong things—and so how could you be successful? Given the anxiety was strong, of course.

Patient: I have to go for another interview tomorrow morning about 10:30, so I can try out these ideas then.

Therapist: Very good. Let's see how you would do it.

Patient: Fortunately, for our discussion, the place of the interview is only about six blocks from where I live . . . it's a small, new firm and they're just getting started and I won't be so awed by them.

Therapist: That's a good start. Now what?

Patient: I can walk there two or three times before the interview time . . . just as you said.

Therapist: And?

Patient: And also talk to myself as you suggested. (Long pause) . . . Come to think of it, I am not as anxious right now about this job interview as I have been about others.

Therapist: Maybe you're getting some feeling about how to handle the anxiety . . . and then, too, you said this was a new, small firm . . . so maybe they don't have the prestige to make you anxious like a big, well-known one would.

Patient: Yes, you have something there.

Therapist: Anyhow . . . back to the issue of tomorrow's interview; let's see what you will, in fact, do.

Patient: Well, I'll get up at my usual time, have breakfast, read the paper and say these things to myself if I feel at all anxious . . . and I assume I will.

Therapist: And if you experience anxiety in the way?

Patient: I'll just talk to myself like we said . . . and keep on walking.

Therapist: Or stop and get a hold of yourself now and then, if you need to. You may notice anxiety more as you approach . . .

Patient: (Interrupting) Yes, I know that . . . I've *noticed* that . . . I always thought I was paralyzed when I left home to go to an interview . . . but as I got closer paralysis turned to death . . . I really died en route (laughs nervously) . . . I really did.

Therapist: You might even want to consider walking toward the job interview place this afternoon . . . if you have time . . . so that you get an even longer run on the problem.

Patient: Yes . . . I can . . . I really can. I'll do that.

Fortunately Margaret was able to make two or three "dry runs" on going for her job interview during the interim between the therapy session recorded above and the actual job interview the next morning. She felt some anxiety—as one would suppose —although she was able to contain it, as she said. Her direct attack on the problem of anxiety in this type of situation illustrates some principles or guidelines that are of value:

1. She picked an easy interview, relatively speaking, on which to try the direct route to her anxiety problems. The firm she was interviewed by was not prestigious and did not have the trappings that made her feel inadequate as much as did ". . . some of the big firms downtown."
2. She practiced going to the place of the interview several times before the actual interview, noting and dealing with the upsurge of anxiety as she discerned it along the way.
3. She added to this direct approach to the anxiety the indirect approach of admitting fully to herself that she was tense and uncomfortable and that this feeling was what she had to deal with, rather than trying to gainsay the feeling. This put her more in direct contact with her feelings which she could not really set aside no matter how earnestly she tried.
4. She learned to see that anxiety is a common and sometimes debilitating part of one's makeup, and that to admit the anxiety and work on it forthright is the best way to handle the problem. As she got further into therapy, there were a number of leads from her past life and past ways of handling anxiety that became intelligible and meaningful to her, but this review of the past did not equip her to deal with anxiety-in-the-present; it only showed she had been neglecting the problem for ages!

Margaret tells a little more of her story:

Patient: I found that advice was really helpful, you know. It really worked—*some*.

Therapist: It really helped *some*.

Patient: Yes *some*—I emphasize that because I still had anxiety but I felt I was in control rather than the other way around. I was doing what I wanted to do—go to the interview, rather than being driven off.

Therapist: And that's real progress . . . so far. I'm cautious too, as it takes a lot of job interviews or anxiety provoking situations for you to be sure you've handled the problem well and in a consistent way.

Patient: I can see that. (Pause) By the way, I think I may have the job I applied for at the little agency down the street. I'll know soon.

Therapist: Excellent. You must have handled things well.

Patient: On the whole, I think I did . . . but you know there were a few times when I was not sure I was in control.

Therapist: I imagine so. What did you do in the clutches?

Patient: Well, the stopping and talking to myself, admitting —*really admitting*—I was anxious and could not and would not escape was very helpful. Also, of course, if I had not directly admitted the problem, I would not have learned what I did . . . but I think I need a heck of a lot more practice. I'm moving!

Therapist: I am sure you are and I'm sure you do . . . but you've made a good beginning.

Patient: I don't know if it would have worked as well at one of the big agencies downtown, though.

Therapist: Perhaps not, but one has to move gradually into the "big time" so to speak.

Patient: Yes, but I don't need them now. (Pause) Know what?

Therapist: No, what?

Patient: Well, I may get into the "big time," as you called it, another way. The firm I may get the job with is really a kind of annex or spin-off from one of the big firms downtown, and this little agency specializes in certain kinds of advertising. But we have to check things out with the downtown office, and so—if

I get the job, it isn't for sure but I think I will, since they asked me how soon I could start—I'll have to go downtown with copy, from time to time, and that will be a challenge for me. I'm excited about that.

Therapist: That does sound encouraging . . . a kind of way of working into the big league through the little league.

Margaret's case illustrates the principles advanced above in relation to direct handling of anxiety. She picked an easy example of a challenge to her confidence (the small advertising agency as contrasted with the ". . . big companies downtown . . ."), and although this was not planned, it worked out well; she made some "dry runs" to the place where the anxiety-provoking situation was most apparent and got used to the idea of being interviewed as she approached the "goal area." She admitted to herself she was tense and untrusting of herself, instead of trying to set all this feeling aside; and she saw more broadly and clearly that she had a general "anxiety problem," which she had doubtlessly had for many years, but had not in the past attacked the problem very well.

WHO . . . WHAT . . . WHEN . . .

In the case of Margaret, matters went pretty well. Sometimes, however, people are less able to pin-point the exact causes of the anxiety, or the specific items that provoke the strongest reactions. Attention to Who, What, When, Where, Why and How are very important and may have to be pursued in some detail before one gets to the point where Margaret was.

WHO? Who makes you anxious? Is it a person in authority? Someone you have had negative dealings with before? Someone who reminds you of another person (even dimly) where there is a residue of unsolved anxiety?

WHAT? What is there about the situation that is upsetting? Is the office too plush? Too prestigious for your simple manner? That was true to some extent with Margaret as she entered executive offices in the well-heeled neighborhood of affluent advertising agencies.

WHEN? When does the anxiety manifest itself most clearly? Or is it present, more or less, all the time? When does it get worse? "When" usually refers to time . . . in Margaret's case it was when she entered the actual office building and again, more clearly, when she entered the specific office of the agency she was applying to.

WHERE? This may overlap some with What and When, but it may be specific, too. Ask yourself, "Where is the anxiety *least* noticed, *most* noticed?" See how these two "where's" contrast with each other; see if there is some similarity such that you can go smoothly from one to the other.

WHY? "Why" is often a weasel word, but we should try to explain it somewhat. The other questions cited above are better than "why" questions, but suffice it to say that "why" questions usually refer to past events that are similar. The reason then why people are anxious now is that they have been anxious in similar situations in the past—a kind of long-range habit pattern. However, in spite of the past, people do learn to solve their problems *here and now*, and so this becomes the dominant theme in overcoming anxiety.

HOW? This "how" question is most important because it leads to "How-do-I-get-over-it?" questions. If we know *how* the anxiety occurs, then we can work toward *how*-it-can-be-overcome; and, of course, that is the whole purpose of this book and of therapy sessions that tackle anxiety in the ways illustrated here. One important "how" question relates to how one deals with the anxiety, and in Margaret's case, she had in the past left the field, run away, bugged-out, so to say. She *maintained* the anxiety-provoking situation for herself by not finding out how to cope; hence each new time around with each anxiety attack, she just gave in, collapsed, bugged-out, and thereby maintained the scariness of the anxiety and of the situation to which it was connected.

People can write down as well as ask themselves verbally the Who-What-When-Where-Why-How questions and answers; and can then analyze them in the manner suggested in the case of Margaret. Upon doing this, they can then bring in assertiveness training, relaxation, writing, imagery and the rest of their armaments to handle the anxiety.

GENERAL CAUTIONS

Some cautions are worthy of contemplating:

1. Avoid acting hurriedly in trying to cope with anxiety. Take time to go through the steps outlined here. You will require concentration and deliberateness; to do the job otherwise is to prejudice yourself against the results.

2. Once you have initiated a direct approach to anxiety management, you may use other approaches and you should select them according to your own preferences, according to the situation, and in relation to how well you can use each of the techniques (relaxation may come easier for you than assertiveness).

3. Be careful in using the direct approach as revealed here, and in over-asserting yourself. If Margaret had gone storming into the advertising agency in an effort to be assertive (actually being aggressive, not assertive), she would have worsened her plight. She needed to take the time to edge up on the problem.

It is always wise to plan your approach to anxiety management. Anxiety is enough of a culprit that it cannot be allowed to run loose. But you must harness anxiety with care . . . otherwise you fail to exert the control you intend and may end up worsening your plight. In fact, it is a fairly good rule that if you are not lessening the anxiety problem you have from one situation to another, or in one type of situation as it reoccurs, you are not using the right techniques, or perhaps you are not using wisely whatever techniques you do employ. Anxiety is a tough customer, but this toughness will yield to your efforts if you are consistent and judicious.

AT THE end of the last chapter (VI), you may have listed some anxiety-arousing situations you wish to tackle directly; now plan how to go about this effort as soon as possible.

Re: ATTACKING ANXIETY SITUATIONS DIRECTLY
Things To Do

1. Using "successive approximations" (a gradual approach), list four or five things you have to do in the next week or two that cause anxiety, and then specify how, in fact, you will approach the matter.

    a. Write a letter applying for a job. Write the letter three or four times to be sure you're comfortable with it.

    b. Practice making a call to a business for a job. Make "dummy" calls first, then go there (part-way, at first, if necessary). Approach the office gradually several times, but don't be driven off by anxiety. Stop and "cool off" by talking to yourself in the way suggested in this chapter.

2. Pick a more remote task that's troublesome—chairing a meeting next fall, arranging a committee, etc., and *outline all the preliminary steps needed to accomplish the goals set.* Then practice these steps, one by one, and be comfortable with each step before going on to the next one.

ADDITIONAL READINGS

Discipline, Achievement and Mental Health, 2nd edition, by E. Lakin Phillips and Daniel N. Wiener, Prentice-Hall, New Jersey, 1972.

How To Be Awake And Alive by Mildred Newman and Bernard Berkowitz, Random Press, New York, 1975.

Creative Coping: A Guide To Positive Living by Julius Fast, Morrow Press, New York, 1976.

The Courage To Create by Rollo May, Norton, New York, 1975.

Chapter VIII

Enlisting the
help of others

Other people have anxiety too! Trade off with them. Help them
with their oppressive problems while they work to assist you.
Since anxiety occurs in interpersonal situations (or is stimulated
by thinking about these situations when you are alone), enlisting
the help of others can be a ready and real source of help.

Several examples of how two people worked to assist each other's
anxiety-reduction can be told in the following cases and excerpts
from therapy sessions. First, the case of John and Mary (fictitious
names), a married couple who had trouble entertaining others
in their home; they became anxious with the task of introducing
people, and in keeping the social evening moving along as they
felt it should. John speaks first in the therapy session:

Patient (John): We both like to entertain; her parents entertained
a lot, so we are both used to it . . . but we just get so uptight
we feel we don't bring it off very well.

**Therapist: And that's been your experience, too, Mary? (Turns to
Mary who is sitting next to John.)**

Patient (Mary): Yes, very much so . . . I get more anxious than

John because I have to prepare the dinner, coordinate everything and see that it all happens as it should.

Patient (John): But I have my share of troubles, although it gets easier as the evening wears on; after I get drinks for the guests the first time—or hors d'oeuvres.

Patient (Mary): But you see my role is a little bit more spread out over the whole situation, the whole evening. And then there's serving the food, keeping it hot, and the final dessert. I don't know why I should have such a time ... my mother never did and I helped her a lot, and I know the ropes. It just upsets me more now to talk about it.

Therapist: I see—when was your latest dinner party and how did it go?

Patient (Mary): We had some people in last Saturday night—just two other couples—and it did go fairly well then—wouldn't you say, John?

Patient (John): Yes, I guess so ... but you know I dropped drinks twice when I tried to hand them to people—I made out like the glass was too wet and slick, but it was really my anxiety, I know.

Therapist: Well, let's take one thing at a time—two bundles of anxiety can be handled a lot better if we can break them down and take them one at a time. What is the first thing that happens that upsets either or both of you?

Patient (John): Well, what gets me first is introducing people who don't know each other. You see, each of us works in large offices quite far removed from one another, and so we have very different friends.

Therapist: Well, let's take the introduction first. Each of you knows the name of your guest?

Patient (John and Mary): Yes, yes, of course.

Therapist: Suppose one of you goes outside the house, rings the door bell and enters, representing one of the guests. Say, "Hello, we're Joe and Susie," and the other of you says, "Welcome Joe and Susie Black." That way, you can usher the people in the house *knowing* their names. Call their names as you greet them: "Hello, Sam, hello, Susan," and try to be firm and confident about it.

Patient (John): We can do that. You know, I can actually forget the person's name when I walk from the kitchen to the front door if I am nervous!

Therapist: I don't doubt it. You'd forget your own mother's name if you were sufficiently upset. So . . . you can practice saying the person's name as you walk to the door, and say it aloud, both of you: "Here come the Smiths—Joe and Nellie," and say it a few times, each to the other.

Patient (Mary): It seems crazy, I know, to forget peoples' names like that . . . but some of the people in my office whom I invite I really don't know that well. Maybe that's the problem.

Therapist: Very well, then . . . we now have the first situation: people appearing at the front door, your stating and remembering their names. Both of you can rehearse this several times before the next occasion.

It was possible to discover six different situations to be worked out between John and Mary in order for them to feel comfortable and without anxiety when they entertained. One was alluded to above: meeting people at the door and stating their names aloud. A second anxiety was that of introducing each new guest or set of guests (usually couples, but sometimes children if the occasion was a picnic on Sunday afternoon) as they were about to mingle with one another. A third problem area was accepting requests for drinks, remembering, filling, and delivering these drinks to the guests. This was the area in which John was mostly working alone because Mary was busy with dinner or with coming in and out to talk with people for short spans of time. Mary could not help John very much with this issue; but both of them could help each other with the greetings and introductions.

Several other issues were: Mary's having the food hot and well co-ordinated with the serving when it came time for dinner; continuing conversation after dinner; and serving after-dinner drinks. One might wonder why John and Mary entertained at all, they had so many problems!

This latter point brings up an additional consideration. It was agreed upon in the therapy sessions that John and Mary would enlist the help of a "favorite couple" to assist them in their anxiety-reduction efforts, and in actual entertaining—they would throw a joint dinner party. This turned out to be a boon to John and Mary in several ways. They had coleaders for the party, itself;

John and his male friend, Fred, both took care of the guests when drinks were ordered, helped each other remember the orders and who ordered them, and sort of buddy-buddied one another through the evening. Mary's friend, Eve, also assisted with the dinner, the way the courses were offered, and how dessert was handled. Enlisting the help of the second couple —Fred and Eve—helped the first couple, Mary and John, immensely with the problems of anxiety in social situations, and it was possible for the therapy itself to provide some new insights for John and Mary as they talked about their problems. Here is an excerpt from a later interview:

Patient (Mary): You know I've been thinking a lot about this problem of social anxiety, now that things are moving along all right—oh, I still get uptight some, now and then, but not to the point that I don't know what I am doing, the way it used to be.

Therapist: What have you concluded?

Patient (Mary): I think I have been competing with my mother who, as I told you, taught me about entertaining in the home . . . dinner parties, and the like.

Therapist: Can you be more specific?

Patient (Mary): Yes. You see, mother was a perfectionist, and I guess I am, too. I can just see her going to the table, arranging everything 5-6—even 10 times, to be sure it was right. She'd have me do things, then come and correct them, and fuss out loud about how my job wasn't done properly.

Therapist: Did she carry this over to the actual guests? I mean worry them, too?

Patient (Mary): No, I think not . . . or maybe I should say I don't really know. The guests always came, and came back, and seemed to have a good time. I think maybe she calmed down after the guests actually arrived—the fussing was about the table setting and the food, not the guests themselves.

Therapist: But this anxiety and fussiness got transferred more generally to the guests in your case—and perhaps in John's case (looking at John)?

Patient (John): I think Mary's point is well taken. I can remember many occasions when I was dating Mary and she had to help her mother before she could go out with me in the evening, and I can see and hear all that fussiness going on. Mary used to complain about how hard it was to suit her mother.

Therapist: So . . . Mary, you are saying what you learned there with your mother was not only how to put on a dinner party—which your mother, anxious or not, was expert at—but you learned to be so anxious to please that you lost sight of the jobs themselves, and certainly lost the pleasure associated with having guests, enjoying them, and entertaining them.

Patient (Mary): That seems to me to be the case. I just never thought about it before—before we came here, that is, and I am inclined to think it has played a big role in my anxiety. (Pause) I don't know about John, though.

Therapist: And you, John? What do you think about *your* problems in this connection?

Patient (John): I don't know . . . I don't have any insights like Mary does; I can't hook things up with the past the way she does. In my family, I rarely witnessed entertainment . . . maybe a friend dropping over to watch a ball game and have a beer with my Dad, or some family members—uncles, aunts, grandparents dropping in—and this was always very informal. I just missed out on being educated in this way, I guess.

Therapist: That makes some sense—you lacked the skills and experiences to make a social evening run smoothly in the manner you both seem to want, but Mary was overtrained, so to speak, and between you two, you could not offer each other very much in the way of support or aid.

Patient (Mary): That does sound fairly right. I often get angry with John and say—"Why can't you remember that?—I've got enough to keep track of already—don't bother me—do it yourself." And so we each fell into the void between us. There's not much mutual help there.

Patient (John): No, I guess not. But working with the L's—Fred and Eve— has made a big difference, and I feel like we are getting a hold of things now. I hope we can help *them* with something sometime.

The case of John and Mary may be a little bit unusual in some ways, but the fact that couples often share the same anxiety-provoking limitations is not uncommon. The couple talking to each other about the issues at hand, understanding each other's limitations and strengths, and enlisting the help of still others, is important and very therapeutic.

Another aspect of the Mary and John problem with anxiety and how it got resolved needs to be illuminated. Mary seemed to have an "insight" about her anxiety, namely, how it was related to what she learned about pleasing others, to what she learned from her mother's behavior which she observed and was part of for many years. This is an insight that Mary achieved after she worked on her own anxiety in practical ways, and, indeed, after she began to emerge from the anxiety; the insight was not a causal factor that unleashed the anxiety and allowed her to function better. The insight, rather, came *after* she had begun to change her behavior. This is an important point for many people who experience anxiety and who want to work on their own problems in this respect. It is important to work on the anxiety in any practical ways available. Working in specific ways is very important and should not at all be replaced by insight or other "uncovering the past" techniques (which may, of course, be useful in their own right).

In John's case there was no insight to the past to resort to—he just had not learned the specific behaviors and skills that were important in certain types of social situations which had become important to him in his marriage. John just had to learn new behaviors; Mary had to tone down her anxiousness over the way she performed behaviors she already knew. The two of them both got relief from a fortunate mutual aid program and from the extra help afforded them through their friends, Eve and Fred.

TWO CASES OF YOUNG MUTUAL HELP

Sue and Helen were two high school girls who, as close friends, discussed their problems with each other and came to find that they had different but still equally compelling anxieties and found a way to help each other with them. Both the girls were interviewed at the same time in order to highlight the manner in which they went about their mutual aid program.

Patient (Helen): Well, you see Sue and I have been friends a long time and we discovered we both had problems of a similar nature, but they took place in different ways.

Patient (Sue): Yes, that's right. I discovered Helen has a terrible time talking with her teachers. My problem is that I have trouble being with boys and talking to them without biting my nails, twisting around a lot and losing my voice.

Therapist: Those are two very interesting problems, although neither one is uncommon. But it is even more interesting to know how you discovered the problems and still more useful to know how you went about helping each other.

Patient (Helen): I never wanted to go see a teacher unless the teacher requested it, or unless my mother went with me.

Therapist: I see, you depended upon others to assist you.

Patient (Helen): Yeah . . . yeah, that's right. I just never could do it on my own. I even had my mother go with me when I picked out my cap and gown for graduation.

Therapist: You felt the teachers would act in unfriendly ways toward you . . .?

Patient (Helen): Oh, no, I liked my teachers . . . I was just nervous when I talked with them or had to go to see them. I never went to them after class no matter how much I didn't understand something . . . I would go around the corridors at school to avoid going near the office for fear of meeting one of my teachers.

Patient (Sue): And you see, I am just the opposite with teachers —I like them and I like to talk with them. It's fellows that I get nervous with . . . and twist my hair and bite my nails and act silly.

Therapist: I see each of your problem areas. Now, can you give me some ways in which you have gone about handling the problems you each feel?

Patient (Helen): Well, you know we were in a speech class that was supposed to help us with our speaking anxieties, and they helped us work on them. . .

Therapist: Yes, I heard about it and I think it is a good way to work on anxieties . . . working with others. Tell me more about it.

Patient (Helen): We each had to designate a way we felt anxious —who made us anxious, what situation did, or something like that? You understand?

Therapist: Yes, I follow you—go ahead.

Patient (Helen): I have this problem with teachers which was hard for me to talk about since I was in a class that had a teacher —naturally it had a teacher—and so . . . and so . . . I was the last one in the class—there were about 35 of us in there—I was the last one to talk about my anxiety. I was so scared when I told the class and the teacher that I was afraid of teachers. Nobody laughed, though.

Patient (Sue): And I was in the class, too, you know. And I told the class about my anxieties with boys, and nobody laughed, not even the boys. I was so relieved.

Therapist: I see the background of your concerns, as you have just briefly reviewed them. Now how did you come to assist each other and how did it work?

Patient (Helen): Well, I can tell my story first (looking to Sue for approval) and then Sue can tell hers.

Therapist: Very well . . . if that's O.K. with Sue (looking at Sue).

Patient (Sue): Yes, that's fine. Go ahead.

Patient (Helen): When the teacher heard me say what I was anxious about, she talked easily and gently with me right then and there and I felt relieved. She asked me some easy questions —like a therapist. She got me to say out loud several times that I was afraid of teachers. I had to say, "I like teachers but I am afraid of them," over and over.

Therapist: And did that help?

Patient (Helen): I think so. At least I felt comfortable with her in the class. She said I should come to her office after class—it was the last period of the day, so I could do that—and when I did we talked a little more. I told her about some specific teachers I was especially afraid of and she and I discussed my feelings a lot. I also came back to see her the next day.

Therapist: That sounds like a good beginning. Anything more before Sue speaks?

Patient (Helen): Yes, Ms. A. gave me an assignment—you might call it that—she said I should go to any one of my teachers and ask a question about the first exam—the exams were coming up in a week or two. So I did that, but I had to go to the math teacher's office—he's Mr. J.—several times before I found him in or before I could get to talk to him.

Therapist: And you finally caught him at the right time and place?

Patient (Helen): Yes, I did, and I stuttered and started over . . . but I got enough courage to ask him and he was pretty nice about it all—not really scarey as I thought he might be.

Therapist: So, by trying out something, you found you could do it? Not perfectly, but at least better.

Patient (Helen): I did. But I was still anxious and I got out of there as fast as I could after the talk with Mr. J. Now I'll let Sue talk because when I came out of Mr. J.'s office I met Sue who was going to work on her assignment and we decided to help each other.

Patient (Sue): The speech teacher said we could team up and help each other if we wanted to. I just happened to come along when Helen came out of Mr. J.'s office somewhat upset, and I told her I was going to try to call one of the fellows in my class who lives near me and see if I could talk to him without getting so upset. We sat down and had a coke and talked about our problems and agreed to help each other, since each of us had a problem the other didn't have.

Therapist: You found each of you was strong where the other wasn't.

Patient (Helen): When we sat and had our drinks, we decided to pick out specific teachers for me and specific fellows for Sue to contact, and we did.

Therapist: And where did you begin?

Patient (Sue): We decided to start with the teachers since we were right there at school. I went with Helen to Miss B.'s room —she's young and pretty and easy to talk to, for me, anyhow,— and we told her what we were doing in our speech class and she understood and wanted to help us. Helen came in and asked Miss B. some questions about an exam and carried on a little conversation. I watched and put in a word or two now and then to reassure her and help her along. We also went over the whole thing again—Helen went out the door and came back in and began the conversation again with Miss B., and I watched like a coach.

Therapist: And that was really helpful, wasn't it?

Patient (Helen): It was, and I was *so* glad Sue was there with me. I don't know what I would have done without her. I just couldn't otherwise . . .

Patient (Sue): Oh, yes, you could . . . you did fine . . . and Miss B. is so nice.

Patient (Helen): Then the next day, we met again and decided that Sue and I would talk to the first boy in the hall that *I* knew and she would chime in when she could, or ask questions, or even say nothing . . . but she was supposed to say something if she could. We found a boy I know quite well—Jimmy, who lives near me and is in some of my classes—and we, or I, started talking to him about his new car and Sue chimed in to ask a couple of questions. She actually carried on a little conversation.

Therapist: And then you both just kept up this business of contacting teachers and fellows and worked on it?

Patient (Sue): That's right, and here we are now telling you about it.

Therapist: I do appreciate that. I wanted to know how you students worked on these anxiety problems in speech class, as the class affords a fine jumping off place to work on anxiety, and I think I can learn a lot from your experiences in ways that will help me with my patients.

Patient (Helen): We hope so . . . only you seem to know more about it than we do.

Therapist: No, not really . . . but I have done this kind of thing with patients before and I have heard of the speech class working on these problems in these mutual ways.

Several talks with Sue and Helen during the semester showed that they both overcame the more formidible aspects of their respective problems—Sue with her anxiety about talking with members of the opposite sex her own age, and Helen with her problems talking with teachers. A talk with the speech instructor, Ms. A., filled in a lot of details that were of interest in studying the general problem of overcoming social manifestations of anxiety in a setting like the speech classroom. The teacher, Ms. A. not only had the members team up in the manner illustrated by Sue and Helen, but would allow the pairs to change partners a time or two during the semester and get experience with two or more "coaches." This proved useful to most students, as they got not only more practice, but also the help of other friends who approached the problem of anxiety-management differently, and added some versatility to their repertoires.

A number of points can be gleaned from the experiences of Sue and Helen in regard to anxiety management.

    1. A classroom setting is a good one in which to approach the problems related to anxiety in various social situations.

2. Students in classes will manifest a number of different —sometimes overlapping, to be sure—anxieties and this will broaden each student's understanding of the commonality of anxieties, how people suffer with them, and how they go about overcoming them. This broadening of experience is a leveler of anxiety in and of itself.

3. The techniques of aiding one another in a buddy-buddy way is valuable, since most of the students would have been reluctant to tackle their personal problems and anxieties so readily on their own. The sharing, the observing of one's own and the other's improvement in anxiety management, acted as a strong reinforcement and encouraged further effort.

4. Bringing back the experience to the classroom setting (the speech class, in this case) also further enhanced the reinforcement value of the buddy-buddy system and the classroom as a forum for reporting on, understanding, and capitalizing on valid efforts at anxiety management. This reference to the setting—the classroom—would be equally good if the setting were a group therapy setting, or any other group where the members, formally or informally, were devoted to a common cause and shared responsibility for this kind of individual undertaking. The fact that many participate, not just the buddy-buddy pair themselves, allows the larger setting to support the efforts of individuals and pairs, and reinforces their gains.

Tom and Jerry (no pun intended) were two athletes who shared a common anxiety bond, as well as an abiding friendship. Both of them played to the galleries, were competitive with one another on the basketball court (more than on the football field which was too large for the audience to capture the antics and humor of individual players), and possessed a *savoir faire* that seemed to say that anxiety was as far from their makeup as the moon.

These two interesting young men were college sophomores when, as a result of a speech class experience similar to that of Sue and Helen, they came together for therapy over concern for their mutual competitiveness and their anxieties. They did not at first see the anxiety of each of them as at least an indirect product of their competitiveness, but this became evident in time. Perhaps many facets of their respective make-up, as well as their competitiveness, made their anxiety at times unbearable; and they seemed to ebb and flow in their experiences of anxiety almost in a pre-arranged way. They tell their story:

Patient (Tom): We came over together—Jerry and I—to see if you could help us. Our speech teacher said you often discussed anxieties more than she did.

Patient (Jerry): Yeah, Tom's right—he and I have a lot in common and we're good friends, but we do have a lot of concern about our anxieties with each other and otherwise. It's gotten worse lately with the start of the basketball season and it's bad for us.

Therapist: Do I understand that each of you is made anxious by the other one? And that the friendship and athletics are carried on in spite of the anxieties each causes the other?

Patient (Tom): Yes, I guess you could say that . . .

Patient (Jerry): (Interrupting)—But you could also say that the friendship and sharing in athletics gets hurt by our anxieties with one another.

Therapist: I see.

Patient (Jerry): Do I make myself clear? Do we make our problem clear?

Therapist: Well, to some extent . . . but there's lots more to know. (Pause) Let me hear when and where each of you is anxious, as you call it.

Patient (Tom): Well, I can only speak for myself. I noticed it a lot in the speech class—the speech teacher referred us, you know —I noticed it most there when I had to talk about athletics and things relating to Jerry.

Therapist: You were not particularly anxious about giving speeches, as such, but only when they touched on athletics or your relationship with Jerry?

Patient (Tom): That's about right—or mostly right. I get very emotional when I talk about Jerry in that way.

Therapist: And you, Jerry?

Patient (Jerry): Well . . . I am anxious in other ways, too, maybe more than Tom, but when we are together with girls, I think I notice it more . . . more than with athletics.

Therapist: You're competitive with one another?

Patient (Tom): Yes, I guess we are . . . but that's normal, isn't it?

Patient (Jerry): I think competitiveness is normal . . . how else can you play and win? I think there must be something else.

Therapist: There may indeed be many "something else's" but I hear some sounds of competitiveness ringing through the din created by anxiety. Can you think about that topic some, each of you?

Patient (Tom): I guess I am competitive, maybe a lot. I guess I want to be high scorer, or get the most rebounds off the opponent's backstop.

Therapist: Does that sound correct to you, Jerry? And are you competitive in a similar way?

Patient (Jerry): Well, yes, but I never thought of it in relation to anything other than the game and winning, what's usual in athletics and sports.

Therapist: It might be that the athletics and sports carry the opportunity for competitiveness—which they certainly do—but more than that, they pit each of you against the other in friendly competition...

Patient (Tom): And I'd like to emphasize the *friendly* part of that . . .

Patient (Jerry): And me too.

Therapist: O.K., I'll take it from you—I won't try to tell you how you feel about the sport . . . but I detect a possibility—only a possibility at this time—that you get pretty angry inside yourselves, so to speak, at one another in the competitive situation and it may go beyond harmless competition in the sporting sense.

Patient (Tom): Well, I doubt it—

Patient (Jerry): (Interrupting) I doubt it, too.

Therapist: O.K., you're both free to doubt this and I want you to say so openly so we can put and keep all cards on the table. (Pause) I think we could examine the anxiety feelings a little more closely, though. When do each of you feel the greatest anxiety?

Patient (Tom): I am not sure. I remember the last game when Jerry moved ahead of me in points scored, and I was taken out by the coach for a few minutes for some advice . . . I was pretty anxious then.

Therapist: Do you think you could have been a little angry too?

Patient (Tom): I didn't notice it that way, but you may have a point as I sat down and cussed out the game and the visiting team—especially one member, a guard—and was upset for a while before the coach could calm me down enough to tell me what he wanted.

Therapist: That sounds like you were angry at several things—being taken out of the game, Jerry moving ahead in points, the behavior of the opponent guard. . .

Patient (Tom): I do have a temper . . . my mother's always after me about it, and so is Dad.

Therapist: Temper . . . anger . . . disgust . . . they are often read as anxiety. They both represent a conflict between the way you *feel* and the way you have to *act*. Being angry at all the things you were angry about, but not being able to act on them—wanting to tell off the opposing guard, wanting to tell your coach not to pull you at that time in the game—all these things bottled up in you, and the result is *anxiety*. (Pause) Make any sense?

Patient (Tom): You mean I was just plain angry?

Therapist: Possibly. It's worth a strong consideration.

Patient (Tom): I guess I never thought about it that way.

Therapist: The basic condition you experience is upset—we call it anxiety in some cases, but in a somewhat different way, it may come from anger which you cannot act on, and that's *anxiety*— at least to some extent.

Patient (Tom): So . . . it's anxiety and anger all mixed up.

Therapist: Sounds mixed up right now, anyhow.

Patient (Jerry): Could I come in here at this point? I have been listening and I see what you're saying . . . I get my upset mostly with girls, especially if Tom and I are around them together, or if we like the same girl.

Therapist: You're suggesting what?

Patient (Jerry): I guess I am seeing some things in Tom's comments that apply to me, but more where girls are concerned . . . less in the sports, you know?

Therapist: You think Tom steps ahead of you, so to speak, with girls, has more "cool," and you feel you may be taking the "second fiddle" position?

Patient (Jerry): Yeah . . . yeah . . . that's right. I see Tom as ahead of me with girls, and maybe I do a bit more scoring—although I don't want to brag—in basketball. (Pause) We each have our specialty.

Therapist: And, in a sense, the specialty, as you call it, may grate some on the other one?

Patient (Tom): You know that may be true, Jerry. What do you think?

Patient (Jerry): I think you may have something there.

This discussion followed this path for another few minutes in the therapy session and in some subsequent sessions. It became increasingly clear that "anxiety = competitiveness" and that added up to one person—Tom or Jerry— being upset with the other one when the other one was seen as getting ahead or as showing some skill or finesse the first one lacked at the moment. Competitiveness was a minute-by-minute matter for them, not an overall matter where they might compare notes at the end of the basketball season, or talk about their relationships with girls. It was a tug-of-war almost all the time they were together—on the basketball court, in social situations with girls.

In spite of this competitiveness, they both liked and respected each other very much, and the anxieties (anger, competitiveness) each caused the other did not destroy the friendship. In fact, the competitiveness and friendship fueled each other—they both liked the edge brought on by first one and then the other moving ahead, in a momentary competition. The rub came in when, on occasion, the anxiety got too far ahead of their friendship and sportsmanlike competitiveness. That's when they each felt the need for help, and this need, or sensitivity, curiously enough, arose in a neutral situation—the speech class.

Several points can be made about the case of Tom and Jerry in relation to anxiety:

1. Anxiety can arise in a so-called normal or commonly non-anxious situation. Competition over girls and excellence in sports are normal—but they can be overdone, and possibly were, at least on occasion, by Tom and Jerry.
2. The speech class setting—a neutral one for both of these young men—was the setting in which the problem was "discovered," and this lead to the more inquiring interest in the anxiety through therapy. When we least expect it,

our anxieties show; and we need to take a lesson from
this fact.

3. The basis of competitiveness between Tom and Jerry was,
itself, normal. No one would want to change or destroy
that; they just needed to understand the limits of their
tolerance for the competitiveness and skill of the other
—Tom with a slight edge in sports, and Jerry with a slight
edge in relationships with girls.

Later on, near the end of the therapy sessions, Tom and Jerry decided to try to play down the excessive competitiveness and to
try to help one another whenever anxiety presented itself to
either of them. Last seen, they were firm friends, more gentle
with each other, more willing to talk over differences they might
have had on the playing field or with girls. Their case represents
to some extent how anger and resentment can register as anxiety;
and how the anxiety develops when differences between them,
arising out of their competition with one another, did not get
cleared up by their "talking out" those differences. The complications that arise are legion when people do not talk out their
differences, not the least of which is a clear manifestation of
anxiety.

The case notes presented on Tom and Jerry show that their talks
with the therapist identified the source of their anxiety—their
competitiveness and the anger (and perhaps jealousy) that arose
therefrom. The therapy, as far as it was carried in these notes,
was mainly a matter of *identifying* the source of the anxiety;
the therapy, as recorded here, did not get into assertiveness,
relaxation procedures or the like. In many ways, both Tom and
Jerry were ready for a more equitable and less anxious relationship between themselves, and the therapy was simply an early
assist in identifying the problems; after that, they moved very
promptly to solve their own problems and, in their particular
case, did not need to give a lot of attention to relaxation, assertiveness, and so forth.

PERFORMANCE ANXIETY

One of the most common instances of anxiety is what we call "performance anxiety." This occurs before giving speeches or committee reports (which we have discussed some—see Chapter III),
but more importantly, before a performance in the sense of

singing, playing in a recital, acting, and so on. These instances of anxiety are legion and even the most experienced performer evidences some anxiety before an appearance. Some performers even have rituals they go through, in a kind of superstitious way, that tend to reduce their anxiety (they think) and insure a better performance. One pianist who appeared on the concert stage not infrequently—although he was not "big time,"—refused to go on stage, or at least felt he couldn't do so, unless he dressed with a certain routine and wore clothes of a certain color. Baseball players—especially pitchers—and other performers are sometimes noted for the little rituals they go through before the game, or even during the game. Not to engage in these preparations or rituals often leaves the performers exposed to anxiety, they each feel; and by the same token their rituals act to suppress or control anxiety in their performance situations.

There are a number of more mundane things you can do if you are prone to anxiety in performance situations. Take, for example, a pianist who is preparing for a recital and has previously become so anxious that he could not perform and has often refused to go on stage. If you were that pianist you might review the material in Chapter III to refresh your memory; but here, however, you ought to focus on the following comments on anxiety control. Maybe they will help you discover some things for your own benefit.

1. Master the selection(s) to be played in the most comfortable setting possible (your own home, studio, etc.).
2. Make tape recordings of your best performances in the preferred setting. Study them well enough to fully appreciate the strong and weak aspects of the performances; this effort really describes your best performance to yourself.
3. Practice in the new setting, where the recital is to take place. The emphasis is on *practice*—don't go first to the new setting and try to play perfectly the to-be-rendered recital pieces; begin with informal practice.
4. When you feel ready, then begin to play the recital piece(s), but not until full readiness is present. Record these efforts and compare to the earlier, natural setting, renditions.
5. Iron out the flaws of the performance in the new (recital) setting before attempting another recording (a recording should be a "best effort").
6. Continue to practice and recite in the recital setting, giving yourself enough time—perhaps several days, if possible—to

get used to random events in the new environment (work-
men around, noises on the roof, the swish of curtains in the
wings, etc.), so that they will not disturb you when the
"real recital time" comes.

7. Continue to work between the old or natural setting and
the new, recital setting, until they are essentially not different in any important way. The same is true for the use of
different instruments (pianos, for example); these must be
seen by you, the performer, as essentially the same. (If you
are a singer or play an instrument other than a piano, the
latter comments are perhaps less relevant.)

8. Gradually bring in people to listen, in both settings, but
especially in the recital setting. Most musicians and performers are not at all anxious if they perform alone—without
an audience. At what size audience they become anxious
is moot, and probably different for different people. But
there is a threshold beyond which anxiety accumulates
rapidly and it is important to know this and to prepare
for the criterion performance (the recital) by adding on
listeners or spectators until you are comfortable with any
number of people. This may be an unwieldy matter to
arrange, but it is less of a problem than being unable to
perform, or having your performance cut short, due to
anxiety.

In short, then, a number of techniques may be employed to lessen
anxiety in performance situations. People who have little or
no anxiety with performance will look upon the measures cited
above as burdensome and superfluous; but for the anxiety-
ridden, no cost is too great to spend to overcome anxiety.

CHILDREN MANIFEST ANXIETY TOO

Children may need help with their anxieties as well as adults. A
number of situations exist where children feel compelling anxiety but do not know what it means—adults do not often know
very well, either, as we have seen—and therefore have no way
of communicating it or moving to overcome anxiety. If adults
do not see the anxiety in the child, this leaves the burden on the
child; and this may account for many instances of where children
withdraw from social contacts, school, peer relations, etc., with-

out apparent reason. Applying our earlier "formula"—see Chapter I—the anxiety is felt at a point where the stress is greater than the pleasure or relief in a situation; where, in a more technical way, the reinforcement of withdrawal or escape behavior is stronger than the reinforcement related to approach behavior.

What can you do to detect anxiety in children? Several things may be picked up by adults without trying for an exhaustive survey or assessment of the child:

1. When a child is very reluctant to engage in activities children usually relish (or the particular child has relished before).
2. When the child is lost for words or other actions once in a situation (say, visiting in a strange home), whereas the child behaves normally at home under similar circumstances.
3. When a child's behavior at home is markedly different when company or particular people visit. There may be something in the overt behavior of a visitor that signals anxiety to the child.
4. When a child refuses to attend school and is possibly diagnosed as a "school phobia" case. The matter here is probably one of anxiety building up in an approach-avoidance way (see Chapter I) with the height of the avoidance (escape) motivation centered in the school itself (or in the classrooms).
5. When a child has trouble sleeping, other than in connection with illness or discernible disruption of the child's routine.
6. When a child is listless, unresponsive, irritable, etc., except, of course, in connection with known illness or other sufficient causes. (If no sufficient cause can be detected, anxiety may certainly—and should—be considered as the important factor in the child's behavior.)
7. When a child seems to give up suddenly and completely on a playmate for no known reason, other than when children have their normal "spats" and withdraw temporarily.
8. When parents feel they have to "be after" the child too much to perform ordinary routine matters, owing to the child's persistent disinterest and adamant disinclination. This is often hard to differentiate from momentary anger, resentment, or disinterest on the child's part, but the amount of time the child behaves in this general way and the resourcefulness of the parents have to combine to make a judgment about whether the child's anxiety requires attention.

There are other criteria that can be employed in determining the extent to which a given child has problems related to anxiety management and how these problems influence daily living. One cannot here produce exhaustive criteria for such a decision; a practical approach is required. The judgment of teachers, psychologists, social workers, or psychiatrists may need to be resorted to in unusual circumstances, but it is well for the parents to exercise as much judgment as possible and to learn from the child's own evaluations in this respect.

We turn attention now to many small matters which may plague you, matters that you tend to tolerate without stopping to see how annoying they may actually be. The next chapter concerns the "little problems" engendered by anxiety, problems that should invite your attention.

THERE ARE probably some people whom you can engage to help you with some of your anxieties; and others you can help. Think about this and then attempt to put it all in practice.

Re: ENLISTING THE HELP OF OTHERS
Things To Do

1. Think of how you and a friend can help one another with a mutually shared anxiety problem or with two different problems where each one knows how to solve one of the two problems well. Agree to discuss each problem with the other person, set up a method of attack (like those outlined in this chapter), and enlist the other's help. Each of you should do this for the other one.

ADDITIONAL READINGS

Scripts People Live: Transactional Analysis of Life Scripts by Claude M. Steiner, Grove Press, New York, 1974.

Creative Coping: A Guide to Positive Living by Julius Fast, Morrow Press, New York, 1976.

I'm OK—You're OK by Thomas A. Harris, Avon Publishers, New York, 1967.

The Book On The Taboo Against Knowing Who You Are by Alan Watts, Vantage Press, New York, 1972.

Chapter IX

Passivity and anxiety

All anxiety does not arise alone from trying to do things and then experiencing frustration and failure; some anxiety comes from inaction and then having to face demands you are unable to meet (or don't want to meet).

In earlier chapters we talked about assertiveness and how important it is in overcoming anxiety; that importance remains. In this chapter we have you underscore the fact that you may not know you are underassertive or passive, so if we turn attention to *passivity*, as such, you may notice and learn more from your own behavior than you previously did.

You may resort to inaction when faced with anxiety: "Oh, well, it is just better to bow out in such a case," you may say. Or you may think, "I am damned if I do and damned if I don't, so I'll take the lesser risk and just do nothing." There are many ways in which your passivity may discount effort and give you a momentary composure which may not last very long.

Passivity can and should be differentiated from assertiveness and aggressiveness. Sometimes people moving from passivity to more assertiveness first become aggressive, then settle into a more steady assertiveness; they have to find their "sea legs" first.

Similarly, when people tone down aggressiveness, they may lean over backwards too far, and become too meek and under-assertive with their new role. The happy ground between aggressiveness and passivity is that of assertiveness, as can be diagrammed in the Figure below.

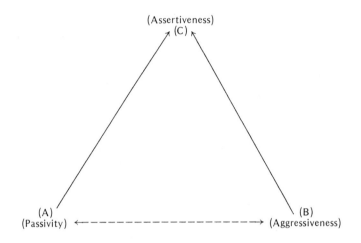

Figure 4. This Figure displays an important relationship between Passivity, Aggressiveness and Assertiveness. A common movement is from (A), Passivity, to (B), Aggressiveness, when at first people try to overcome Passivity too quickly or too drastically. Likewise, one may find the movement from (B), Aggressiveness, to (A), Passivity, difficult. Both of these moves are not as welcome or useful as moving from either (A), Passivity, or (B) Aggressiveness, to (C) Assertiveness; moving to Assertiveness is more nearly ideal and constitutes the basis for many of the messages in this book.

Passivity may take several forms often not recognized as such; the following are common but not complete examples of passivity:

1. *Boredom.* This is a common "ailment" in modern life. Housewives are bored and so take tranquilizers in abundance. Students are bored and thus drop out of school. Business men are bored and take to drinking, gambling, running out on their wives and otherwise stirring up excitement in order to make their stale lives more interesting. Boredom is a failure to see or rise to challenges when they exist; and it is a tendency to "put down" interesting, or

potentially interesting, experiences because they are judged in advance as "meaningless," "trivial," or the like. Boredom is much more a reflection on the person than on the experience itself, that is, if the boredom continues very long or is related to a variety of personal experiences. Boredom is sometimes a plea to others to respond more fully to the bored person; or it may be a kind of veiled threat that if the other person doesn't become interesting soon, the bored one will take off or end the relationship. Boredom, then, takes many forms, or arises out of many conditions; but mostly it is a fairly formidible kind of passivity that often carries with it a kind of "low grade anxiety"—like a low grade temperature—never enough to make one really ill (or disturbed), yet important enough to cause one to lower his/her level of participation socially and to miss out on life's challenges.

2. *Existential Loneliness.* Much has been said recently about existentialism and emotional states related thereto, such as loneliness, ennui, and so on. This phrase—existential loneliness—adds a kind of philosophical flavor to being lonely, and seems to say that the lonely person has really thought out things and has concluded that loneliness is, indeed, a studied and logical reaction to existence. The philosophical part need not concern us here; what is important is that passivity often leads to loneliness. If people are to remain active with other human beings, they need others' concerns and interest and, therefore, have to be ready, willing and able to reciprocate and carry their responsibility for half, or nearly half, of the interaction. Lonely people often assume that it is up to the other person to approach them —"If they want me, they'll call . . . or let me know somehow," one anxious and lonely person averred. Sometimes lonely people make a token approach to others, but do so with an undertow of feeling that the others don't want to be friendly, hence they make a frail effort that comes over like a lead marshmallow; then the lonely ones go back into their loneliness saying, "See, they don't want to be friendly." Loneliness, if it is carried on very long, or if it is not just a temporary reaction to a specific loss from death, divorce, separation, job loss, etc., is a kind of self-fulfilling prophesy: People get the reaction they anticipate, then say to themselves or others: "See, it is just like I said it would be."

People in this state of affairs display a chronic state of anxiety, because whenever the issue of activity, approaching others or showing assertiveness comes up, they denounce it as too much trouble, as futile, or as falling on deaf ears. Reinforcement through escape and non-participation is the common story here; not reinforcement through participation and relating to others.

3. *Failure To Follow-up On Agreements Made With Others.* Many times we harbor low grade anxieties owing to not keeping our word with others. We often rationalize such decisions and actions, blame others, saying the agreement was not worthy of keeping, and so forth. But the fact remains that if we have anxiety, we retain some feeling that we should have kept the agreement; there is *conflict* present. We cannot rid ourselves of the restive feeling; we cannot dismiss the concern. The absence of being able to set the issue aside is, itself, anxiety; and it will likely continue until some resolution has been reached. The anxiety will always remain subject to reactivation when we see the person or have some reminder of the agreement. This kind of anxiety may arise in connection with borrowing something and not returning it; with accepting invitations but not reciprocating; with an intended promise to respond in some specific way to another person but not following up on it; and the like. These are not terrible transgressions, nor are they the basis for major guilt reactions; but they do signal anxiety, an anxiety that often acts like a "low grade fever," giving us a generally uncomfortable feeling which is not easily dissipated. The obvious solution is to carry out the intended: Make the call, return the book, extend the invitation; for only with these *overt* efforts will we feel we have fulfilled the obligation which is the basis of the anxiety and the underlying conflict. Just trying to dismiss the whole matter out of hand will probably not work.

4. *Push-Pull Relationships With Others.* Sometimes passivity results from a strenuous, on-again, off-again or push-pull relationship with another person. This kind of *conflict* results in a feeling of not knowing where you stand with someone. One day things are fine and you think you can build on them; the next day, they turn around one-hundred-eighty degrees, and you don't know where you stand. After

a while this pattern of "sometimes yes, sometimes no," begins to dominate the relationship and you tend to lapse into passivity. If, for a while, the relationship *appears* better, you have the undertow of feeling that it won't last, so why put forth effort—this results in passivity and resignation. On the other hand, when the relationship really shows itself to be poor or unreliable, you know you cannot depend upon it; again, you turn to resignation and a what's-the-use feeling. Either way, up or down, you get disenchanted. These situations tend to be chronic and to ultimately result, in most instances, in a severing of the relationship—this predicament being common in marriage problems before separation or divorce, in other man-woman relationships, and in many friendships of a non-romantic or non-sexual nature. The continuing conflict makes for considerable anxiety: Conflict spells uncertainty and unreliability in the relationship, and this adds up to a more or less chronic state of anxiety. The remedy here is to see first if the relationship has any long-range stability and to decide whether to halt it altogether or try for a more restricted relationship that can develop some dependability by reducing the vacillations and conflicts. If the latter decision fails, the relationship is probably not worth the anxiety—even when it was "good"—so a severing is probably called for. On the other hand, a good assertive try and some relaxation practice in the face of anxiety *might* help you bring the relationship around to an enjoyable and stable level; only you can try to pull the relationship out of the muck and mire, and only you can judge the results.

Failure to act on a level appropriate to your ability, interest and opportunity may also result in passivity. Every day each of us is confronted with the opportunity to rise to a number of demands, and seldom can we rise to all of them; we have to pick and choose; we have to have priorities. In this complex interplay with our personal and interpersonal environment, we have to decide whether the extra social engagements are worth the price we pay in time, money, energy; whether the job opportunity has too many drawbacks in spite of the salary and promotional enticements it offers; whether we need to take the time to go back to school, serve on important committees, join groups for sake of job or family; and so forth. Sometimes we are confronted with just too many such choices and we become emotionally or psychologically impoverished amidst plenty. In such cases, we tend to back off, refuse to participate at all, and just feel burdened beyond control. The occasional answer to overstimulation and an oversupply of opportunity is retreat and passivity—we just have to sleep it off.

Also connected with this situation is often the feeling that too much success is as much an "illness" as too much failure; and true this may be. Success can spoil as surely as failure, if success makes for a chronic disequilibrium in one's overall living patterns. Part of our life, in this case, becomes too important, results in failure in the rest of our life—the tail begins to wag the dog, and when this happens too often or for too long a time, the wagging tail becomes weary and cannot carry the burden. A passive anxiety state results.

Reevaluating priorities, reassessing where we are going, reexamining our potential in the face of multiple demands and opportunities, are needed to get out of the anxiety bind. This situation may take all the help we can get from all the anxiety-reducing techniques provided here.

INERTIA AND ANXIETY

People reporting on anxiety of a low-grade but continuing nature may find that they cannot bring themselves to do things they think or feel they want to do; they just can't get up the energy to go see that movie; they can't find a way to go see the children perform at school or on the playground; they can't go pick up the books at the library they know are reserved for them, and the like. These kinds of situations produce guilty reactions, too, since people basically want to do the things they are interested in, but lack at the moment the initiative to "get on the stick." They have the opportunities but lack the behavior to take advantage of them. Their guilt, then, turns in to anxiety and produces a persistent gnawing feeling of their inability to reach out. Stewing then in their juices is most unpleasant and unrewarding and often invites the criticism and even the scorn of others.

Enlisting the help of others—see Chapter VIII—may often be useful in getting you, like those people, over the threshold to action. Role playing, in the sense of talking to another about your impasse and using the discussion to lead to small actions, may be useful in getting you started. Go pick up the phone—in a role-playing way—and make a dummy call to the library for the book, or make the reservations for the play you want to see— then act on this first attempt. You will find that the role-playing can help overcome the inertia and can put you through the exact paces you need to become active. You can then go, relay fashion, on to other activities, and the first thing you know, you will be solving your passivity and anxiety problems by and through real action.

EACH DAY DO SOMETHING YOU *WANT* TO DO

People sometimes report they have no interests and there is nothing they really want to do. Of course, this is really not possible, unless they are at the point of death or totally disabled; people do have interests—they just need to learn better ways of observing and acting on them.

Helping you get out of passivity in this sense can be done by making a list of things you ideally would like to do, even though there are limitations, difficulties and extenuating circumstances. Say to yourself: "Each day I am going to do just one thing I want to do." No matter how trivial it is, do it! All of us have the little secret corners of our lives we occasionally examine, then close up because we think doing what this secret thing calls for is impossible or unwise. (We are not talking about doing things injurious to others, or illegal things; but aside from these limitations, there are many little corners we could sweep the cobwebs off and look at squarely.) These small things we really want to do may be as simple as buying a tool we need but have not tried to afford; calling up an old friend and meeting him for lunch; going and looking at, or trying out, a car we want to buy but feel is too extravagant for us to own; going to an "x-rated" movie; buying some food or clothes (those patent leather shoes!) we want but feel embarrassed to tell others about; and doing more things than we ever realized existed in our little "mental closets."

Doing these things gets us out of a rut, breaks the passivity impasse and shows us how possible the impossible is! Yielding to passivity is a very restrictive way to live, and it harbors more anxiety than can possibly come from all the arguments, catastrophes and emergencies we will have in a life time. We understandably watch for the big anxiety producers, and well we should; but at the same time, we ought to be aware of the countless minutia that produce and maintain the anxiety that encompasses so many of us too much of the time.

EACH DAY DO SOME THINGS YOU *DON'T* WANT TO DO

There are also things you don't want to do (don't say "Can't do" —be honest and admit that you "Don't want to . . ."), and these must be attended to as well. You may hover between the things you want to do but feel you can't and the things you don't want to do and feel you should. What a way to live! All bottled up, coming when you should be going, going when you should be coming.

How to straighten it out?

First, do the thing(s) you don't want to do. This may sound silly to you because doing what you want to do is much easier. You tell yourself, "I'll do this easy thing first (the thing I want to do but have not had the courage to do) and then I'll do the hard thing." It just won't work that way. Chances are you'll fool yourself again. You may do the easy things but you'll wonder at the same time if you can do the hard one(s), and you may not get around to them. Then you'll feel guilty again, and start all over the confusion between doing what is needed and what is primarily pleasurable.

The problem is not unique and you have to simply begin to think about what you're doing.

There is good sense in doing the hard things *first*. Although it might be unpopular, discipline yourself for the harder tasks, then go for the easier ones. There is a principle here. Of two activities—one cherished and one not—take the lesser one, the one you're disinclined to do, the one that's hardest to do, and do it first. Then *reward* yourself with the easier, lovelier, more enjoyable task. That's the way it works. You get a kind of double dose of reward or reinforcement: one for doing the difficult thing ("There, I did it!"), another for the already enjoyable thing. If you turn the tasks around, you may get the enjoyment (reward, reinforcement) for the easy or enjoyable thing you've done, BUT it may erase the guilt feeling that you cannot, will not (and "Oh, isn't it a shame?" to leave off there) do the harder things. You risk continuing the conflict, and you continue the anxiety. That's no way to run your life if you want to control and manage anxiety effectively!

Doing the harder things first, and then following with the easier go a long way toward overcoming passivity. This method helps with self control, strengthens the "weaker" behavior so that it becomes easier to manage later, and also keeps the rewardable (reinforceable) behavior going strong, which is what you need for overall self control.

WE ARE ALL passive in some ways. How can you overcome your passivity—very concretely —where you think it is not a good practice for yourself? Write down these examples and move on.

Re: PASSIVITY AND ANXIETY
Things To Do

1. Note the time and relationships when you think you have been the most passive, assertive or aggressive.

    Passive: When I _____

    _____

    Assertive: When I _____

    _____

    Aggressive: When I _____

    _____

    What would you like to change or continue about each of these situations? In terms of the chapters of this book state (write down) how you can overcome passivity in some situations, how you can reduce aggressiveness, and how you can continue and/or extend assertiveness in important ways. Be specific and try out your efforts *today.*

ADDITIONAL READINGS

How To Be Awake And Alive by Mildred Newman and Bernard Berkowitz, Random Press, New York, 1975.

I'm OK—You're OK by Thomas A. Harris, Avon Publ., New York, 1967.

How To Make It With Another Person by Richard B. Austin, Jr., McMillan Press, New York, 1976.

Own Your Own Life by Richard Abell, McKay Publ., New York, 1976.

The You That Could Be by Fitzhugh Dodson, Follett, Chicago, 1976.

Power! How To Get It, How To Use It by Michael Korda, Random House, New York, 1975.

Chapter X

Don't ignore the "little problems" of anxiety

It is often the little things in life that trip us. We prepare for the big events, try to watch carefully where we are going, only to fall over the minutia of everyday life. This is reflected in the Frances Crofts Cornford poem:

A young Apollo, golden-haired,
Stands dreaming on the verge of strife,
Magnificent, unprepared
For the long littleness of life.

The "long littleness of life" may be composed of many short episodes that trigger our anxiety reactions. We need to take a look at these.

BLUSHING. While blushing may often be amusing or even coy, it may also show anxiety. This is not usually a serious anxiety reaction insofar as it affects others; and it may not cause a lot of subjective concern to the one who is blushing. But frequent blushing or repeated blushing on given topics (say, sensitivity to sexually tinged remarks or jokes) may add up to a considerable amount of anxiety over time. Some anxiety reaction to the blushing itself may result. If you are inclined to blush easily, the first corrective measure would be to note the topic or topics about which you blush; and secondly, how often this characteristic seems to occur. If the two note-takings are closely related, you may have a problem with anxiety occasioned by blushing.

Blushing is most commonly related to sexual topics, "dirty" jokes, and sexual innuendos. You may also blush when confronted with a remark by another person disclosing something you have considered private or secret; in this instance, you may later show anger or disgust at the person for having transgressed on a matter of confidence. Generally, blushing is due to a conflict between what you privately think or wish to be true in contrast to some public or social utterance on the part of another person. You do not cause yourself to blush through conflict, but blushing is a reaction to the conflict between what you hold to be true (or want to be true or what you consider appropriate) and the contrasting comments or verbal pronouncements of another person. Like all other forms of anxiety, blushing arises in a conflict situation. But there are ways to handle this kind of anxiety and the underlying conflict just as there are ways to handle other anxieties we have discussed in this book.

The tendency toward too much blushing may be handled by talking to a friend about this habit and trying to explain to him/her just why you think you blush too much. Get the friend's reactions, too, because it may provide a clue to why you blush, and also additional information on the social impact your blushing has on others. Another remedy for too much blushing is for you to tell the jokes or repeat the conversation to others that made you blush in the first place. The matter of repeating the incidents with an intention to defuse the anxiety, will help extinguish the anxiety reaction and make you less prone to the blushing on later occasions. Anxiety from or related to blushing occurs in a social setting—you never heard of anyone blushing while alone, did you?—and thus its cure, so to speak, has to be forged in a social context.

Talking to yourself about your tendency to blush may be of help. The limitation on talking to yourself about blushing is that you may not be able to capture the social context adequately. But paying attention to your imagery (see Chapter IV) will help when dealing in a solitary way with blushing. Also, writing down the fact that you have a tendency to blush in such-and-such a situation often helps to identify the circumstances better and therefore to preclude the blushing. The most satisfactory antidote to blushing, however, lies in dealing with blushing in a social context; and in trying to reduce the anxiety that is associated with some tenter-hooks topic (e.g., sex) that seems to bring on the blushing.

EMBARRASSMENT. Embarrassment is usually less of a social problem, hence it produces less anxiety than blushing. Blushing comes on unexpectedly, but embarrassment is often readily admitted by the embarrassed person. We face embarrassment when some contrast appears between what we said and what we did, or between what we predicted (or wanted to be true) and what happened. There is, indeed, conflict here, but it is usually more readily absorbed and dealt with than most other instances of conflict that result in binding anxiety.

Sometimes people are not willing to meet embarrassment head on; they thereby worsen the conflict and resultant anxiety. The poet captured this condition when he said:

Jack was embarrassed—never here more,
And as he knew not what to say, he swore.

In such an instance we turn manageable embarrassment into further complications and may be unable to wiggle out of the embarrassing situation. Anger may result.

If embarrassment is characterized in large measure by conflict, and if embarrassment results in a lingering anxiety (if the embarrassment is not admitted and dealt with openly), then you can cope with it in ways similar to those used in coping with other anxieties. These will, of course, include checking your *assertiveness* (you may find your embarrassment comes from being too aggressive, not constructively assertive); instituting some *relaxation procedures* to deal with the embarrassment (especially if you know that at some forthcoming meeting you will be confronted with things said or done that form the basis for your embarrassment at the hands of your critics); and *writing* down several ways to handle the embarrassment. These may prove to be effective antidotes to the embarrassment which you will later have to admit and cope with openly.

PREOCCUPATION. Preoccupation is a more passive and private psychological condition than either blushing or embarrassment; yet it is one of life's little, nettling things that both signals anxiety and leads to more anxiety. When you are preoccupied, you may of course be concentrating on an important matter;

or you may be *pre*-occupied, meaning you are trying to settle some conflict in your mind and you are so concerned with it that other important things are missed. Preoccupation implies that you are unable to be concerned, or occupied, with other matters; the conflict situation, worry, whatever, preempts your interest and concern and holds you glued to the problem.

Such preoccupation is, itself, a sign of anxiety. Also, you become more anxious, perhaps even angry, when someone tries to shake you out of your preoccupation. You are, in your preoccupation, going over and over the problem, chasing your own mental tail, so to speak, and you dislike having this brought to your attention or being dissuaded from your course.

Preoccupation has a social consequence in many instances: Others note the preoccupation; you note it, also, and may be embarrassed about it; and you fail to attend to other significant matters as a result of the preoccupation. As a result, anxiety accumulates, and you continue to fail to solve the problem which causes the preoccupation.

What to do about it all? As in all instances of handling anxiety and the basic conflict involved, the first thing to do is to identify the elements in the preoccupation: What is the conflict? What do you want to do and not want to do? What did you think (or hope) would happen vs. what did happen? The conflict will be stated in some such terms. Ferret out this conflict, expose the elements to the light of day, then decide how to handle the conflict. It may call for regrouping your efforts, for more assertiveness (and less aggressiveness), and it may call for closer examination of your thoughts, images, hopes, and beliefs. If the problem underlying the preoccupation was brought on by what you said or did—or didn't say or do when you might have—then the problem is equally solvable by something you may say or do in the future. The solution is potentially in your own hands if you identify the elements of the conflict and anxiety connected with your preoccupation. Any number of techniques may work.

Try to go through the techniques developed and discussed in this book—from assertiveness right on through the list—and set down how each technique might apply in your particular instance of preoccupation. That is, after you have decided what the conflict underlying your preoccupied is all about. For example:

John was preoccupied with feelings of lacking self confidence in social groups. After he had been to a party, or even after he had participated in "bull sessions" in his rooming house, he had many after-thoughts about what he said, how he felt he appeared to others, what he thought others felt about him and so forth. He would stew for hours, as he put it, after even a most informal meeting with a group of peers. In his therapy, he and the therapist decided upon a trial period using assertive training as the main therapeutic thrust. His session went like the following:

Patient: You see . . . as I said last week, I am always plagued by feeling that others don't like me, or that they think I am nutty or stupid.

Therapist: I see. This feeling comes after you've interacted with others in a group, more so than if just you and another person talk about something?

Patient: Yes, I think so. You see, I can always tell what *one* other person thinks, or at least I can ask him and find out that way. But the larger the group, the more anxiety I seem to have.

Therapist: And after the interaction is over, you brood over it—is that right?

Patient: Yes, that's exactly it . . . except that I may brood over it for hours, then even pick it up the next day and go through the whole thing again.

John's therapeutic work centered on assertive training where he learned to introject into these social group situations, ideas, questions, comments and the like and thereby engage in more specific and clarifying interactions with others. He came out of these social discussions more at ease and less prone to be preoccupied. It took some doing, however, but the main thrust in overcoming the preoccupation anxiety was through a more deliberate assertiveness on his part, so that he got better feedback from others and had less to worry about later; he learned where he stood, which balance was generally pretty satisfactory to him.

Another patient—Mary, we'll call her—was preoccupied with how she "shot off her mouth at others" when she was angry or upset with them. She felt she had lost a number of friends by being so curt and had distanced many others. She would "fly off" at someone, then later be quite guilty and preoccupied and worried about what she had said and done. A brief session from her therapy tells us how she handled this problem:

Patient: I guess I'm too aggressive—I fly off at people too easily. I want to learn how to control my temper and get on an even keel more.

Therapist: The temper outbursts not only cause you distress at the time they occur, they also preoccupy you later.

Patient: Yes, that's what I mean, and yes, they tie me up in knots for a long time afterwards . . . then I'm so guilty when I see a person later . . .

Therapist: You carry around a load of anxiety and tension all the time then when you are confronted with something you don't like, you just let go with all your resentment and don't care about the consequences—but later, you worry yourself silly.

Patient: That is a pretty fair statement, I think.

Therapist: But the tension that is with you all the time . . . that may be an important part of the problem that leads you to such hasty belligerence toward others.

Patient: Come to think of it, I am preoccupied all the time . . . not just after a battle with someone . . .

Therapist: If that's the case and also judging from what I see and hear, some efforts at relaxation training might be worth considering.

Patient: Oh . . . how does that work?

Therapist: Well, there are a number of techniques you can learn and practice on yourself to relieve tension.

It is only necessary to say that with her particular preoccupation, Mary was able to effectively use relaxation training to reduce tension, overconcern with herself, her temper outburst and resultant preoccupation. Her over-aggressiveness resulted in her damaging her relationships with others, but the relaxation training assisted her in reducing her general state of tension; hence it also aided her in her across the board effort to gain self-control and self-management.

JEALOUSY. Jealousy is as common as any other human emotion. Like many other feelings, it is related to other people, to conflict with them, and just as often it is related to our own selfish motives. We are jealous of others—which means we feel anxiety in their presence or when we think of them or have to deal with them—when they appear to have something, or do something we want to have (or do) ourselves. We want what they have, or what they appear to have; we feel envy and often wish the worst of luck to them.

Jealousy is frequently thought not to be associated with anxiety, but you have only to look carefully at your next feelings of jealousy to discover that you feel tension and anxiety in relation to the jealousy. If you observe yourself carefully, you will see that you are also in conflict: You want to *appear* free of jealousy, but actually feel differently; you want to ". . . see what the other person has . . ." but also try to avoid the other person so as not to appear too interested; upon hearing what the other person has said or done about which you may feel jealousy or envy, you wish to discount that person's credibility; and so on through many, many conflicting feelings.

The general remedy here is like that of handling any other type of conflict: Define the pros and cons, the approach or positive vs. the avoidance or negative features of your feelings in regard to the person. If you can do this clearly, you have a leg up on the problem, so to speak, and can then begin to handle each set of feelings (both pro and con). You may also find, upon further examination, that you do not assert yourself with this person about whom you feel jealous. Some effort at developing a more forthright stance toward the person may be very desirable. In order to develop this stance, some relaxation and image-probing may be indicated. Do you see yourself in an inferior position in comparison to the person? Do you see the other person having or showing some skill or social presence that you feel you lack and would like to have? Admit this candidly to yourself. Try relaxing as you think of the pro and con features, and make them as specific and detailed as you can in connection with the relaxation.

It is helpful, too, to write down: "Although I envy Sally, I will not let this feeling get in the way of my relationship with her—I'll try to carry on as normally as I can with her." Or, "Although I feel both envy and dislike for John, I will not let these feelings get the better of me—I will treat him as objectively as I can when I next see him." Then proceed, of course, to try to act on these writings. Combining assertiveness, relaxation (together with clearing up your imagery) and writing, can constitute a three-pronged attack on the problem of jealousy or envy. With a little judicious practice, your handling the envied person may be greatly improved, which is to say you can reduce your anxiety to a tolerable level or even to near-zero (none of us can expect to be completely at zero in anxiety about anything!).

It is helpful, too, to confront the *topic* about which you feel envy in connection with another person. If you think Sally dresses more stylishly than you do, or shows better taste in clothes, say to her: "Gee, I like your new outfit—do you mind telling me how you buy clothes so wisely?" This will get you off your own anxiety hook by admitting openly to Sally that you admire her taste in clothes (which deals with your own conflict); and chances are you will feel much better about yourself for having spoken so objectively and successfully to her on that occasion. You may even want to carry on a further conversation!

FEAR OF SUCCESS. Fear of success seems like a *non sequitur*, but it isn't. Fear of success is really part of our old friend "conflict," in which we desire success but feel uncomfortable about the actual *performance* that would lead to success. We want the fruits but doubt if we can engage in the labor successfully; we lack personal confidence in being able to carry off the act but very much feel if we were successful it would be at too great a cost. Another way to put the issue is to ask the question: "Is success worth the effort?"

Implicit also in the feeling of fear-of-success is the notion that the success would not be great enough—no matter how successful you are, you silently or implicitly wish it to be greater, even outstanding! Therefore any level of success short of perfection would be a come-down and that would be disappointing or embarrassing. If you then don't try, you don't have to face success at a level less than that desired. You fear, or have anxiety about, coping with the outcome of your effort. Fear of success, then, is really anxiety about the outcome of your efforts and this, in turn, is based on conflict.

Coping with this situation, once you realize the nature of the conflict, is not too difficult: You state as clearly as you can to yourself (orally or in writing) what the pros and cons are about the *level of success* you require, decide if you can really shoot that high, then maybe modify your expectation downward, and try out your luck in the real situation. Once the discrepancy between what you desire (or expect or wish) and what you are actually able to do is understood and reduced, you can then act comfortably and accept the outcome for what it is. In other words, you avoid over-estimating (or over-expecting) and learn to accept the outcome. When you have done this, you reduce anxiety and you no longer fear success. Above all, you have learned to estimate yourself—your real performance—more carefully and modestly against your aspirations, and that's no small accomplishment!

HELTER-SKELTER ANXIETY. Sometimes people are so anxious to please others, to do "what is right," and to be ready to respond to social demands, that they are in a constant dither. Their behavior makes a comedy of being adequate. You might think of a hostess at a dinner party—always forgetting to put something on the table, always just about to get there but never really quite arriving. . . This is a helter-skelter-pell-mell acting person who appears wound up and overactive, often over-talkative, and visibly anxious. Too much company with this helter-skelter person is wearing and boring. Ask yourself if you appear this way very often, or occasionally, or only when you are especially anxious to please.

The person acting this way is always in conflict, too. The conflict is between trying to please others and having strong self-doubts about the pleasing, about the outcome. The self-doubting is constantly checked out and up-dated, so to speak.

If you have this kind of problem, even on occasion, try to figure out who and for what reasons you are anxious: Is there someone you especially want to please or impress? Is there some feeling that what you have or do is not good enough for others? Is there some blemish, so to speak, on you or your manners, or your surroundings that you fear will be detected or not approved? Are you afraid that others will "discover" something about you that you have to cover up with an anxious effort to please?

If you can identify what you are asserting, what you are trying to do, if you can put your finger on your real feelings here, you can make the first step in overcoming the problem. If you make this identification, you can then practice relaxation and say to yourself: "I don't have to prove myself to anyone—I am O.K." Or, "I am madly trying to impress—I don't have to do that—they can take me as I am." Going over such statements, together with relaxation practice could be very helpful.

A further effort might be extended to the actual environment in which you feel the anxiety, the helter-skelter feeling. Say it is in your home when you have guests in, either formally or informally.

Try acting a kind of "dummy role" whereby you imagine others are coming to visit and you practice talking to them, serving them drinks or "goodies" in a relaxed way. If you feel yourself getting wound-up, stop, start over with the activity, and keep on in as relaxed a manner as possible until you have finished that activity. Do this on several occasions and for several kinds of activities—serving drinks, serving snacks, serving dinner, keeping conversation going, and the like. Once you have been over these kinds of activities in an orderly and relaxed way, you will see that you can drop the helter-skelter manner and live more comfortably. If another person puts too much of this kind of anxiety on you—imposes it on you—you can just say to such a person—"Relax, I can get it myself." Or "Don't try too hard to please me—I can make out all right on my own."

If you find any of the "little problems" presented in this chapter are anxiety characteristics that you typically have, or sometimes show, you can move very deliberately to overcome or greatly reduce them. You have but to discern the nature of the conflict underlying embarrassment, envy, helter-skelter behavior, and so forth, and then proceed by assertiveness, by relaxation, or other methods to bring the conflict under control. Your reward is reducing anxiety, knowing that you can handle your own problems, and having daily proof that more comfortable living is a reality for you.

> GET OUT your notebook or pad and jot down several "little problems" you have likely been ignoring; decide what to do.

Re: THE "LITTLE PROBLEMS" OF ANXIETY
Things To Do

1. Make a chart for all seven days of the week thus:

	Sun.	Mon.	Tues.	Wed.	Thurs.	Fri.	Sat.
blushing							
embarrassment							
pre-occupation							
jealousy							
fear of success							
helter-skelter anxiety							

Put in an "incident" wherein you blushed, were embarrassed, feared success, etc. Also, put in the person's name with whom you were interacting at the time.

2. Then write down separately for each incident what you *could have done differently* in each anxiety-provoking situation. Use relaxation, writing technique, or other methods studied in this book to cope with the provocation. Then, the next time around—there surely will be a "next time"—note how you've improved (usually modestly, gradually) and try to begin to build on your initial step forward in anxiety control.

ADDITIONAL READINGS

Anxiety and Stress by Harold Borowitz et al., McGraw-Hill, New York, 1955.

The Experience of Anxiety: A Casebook, Oxford Press, New York, 1963.

The Psychology of Anxiety by Eugene E. Levitt, Bobbs-Merrill, Indianapolis, 1967.

The Courage To Be by Paul Tillich, Yale University Press, New York, 1952.

Short-Term Psychotherapy and Emotional Crisis by Peter E. Sifnoes, Harvard University Press, Cambridge, Mass., 1972.

Short-Term Psychotherapy and Structural Behavior Change by E. Lakin Phillips and Daniel Wiener, Prentice-Hall, Englewood Cliffs, New Jersey, 1966.

Chapter XI

Recapitulation

This book boils down to a number of statements about common conditions in your experiences that lead to anxiety reactions. Since we are all more human than anything else, we all experience some amount of anxiety in a variety of situations, depending on how able we are to cope with the situations and the anxiety they engender. Any amount of anxiety is unwelcome if we cannot cope with it; various amounts of anxiety are tolerable if we have ways of coping. The main purpose here has been one of finding ways of managing anxiety, which is to say of keeping it from getting the better of you.

One important message is that it is the entire person—*you*, the whole *person*—who is anxious; your physiology, your psychology, and the social situations in which you find yourself. You have to handle your anxiety by recognizing this fact and going on from there.

There are many ways in which anxiety can be better managed. Some ways are not effective—trying always to ignore your feelings, hoping they will just go away, or hoping that somebody else or something else will relieve you of your discomfort. There are other ways—ways you can learn easily or ways you may already know to some extent—that can be very effective in handling anxiety.

This book has elaborated on the effective ways of managing anxiety in daily life. These ways may be summarized briefly: *Assertiveness* (knowing who you are, what you want, knowing your rights, feeling good about asserting yourself); *Relaxation* (developing techniques of muscle and whole-body relaxation which can reduce anxiety and lead to more effective assertiveness); knowing yourself better subjectively (your *Imagery* and how it influences you, how it places a kind of stamp of approval or disapproval on you, and how it arises from your success or lack of it in life); using a time-and-tried method of identifying your objective and developing self-control through *Writing*; learning how to *temporarily stay away* from commonly experienced anxiety-provoking situations without forfeiting your anxiety management potential; knowing how to *directly attack anxiety-producing* situations and encounters with some skill and confidence; seeing how you can *enlist the help of others*; and being fully aware of the many *little anxiety arousing situations* that may not devastate you but which nonetheless, if they go uncontrolled, may make living a good deal less enjoyable.

All of the instances of anxiety are based, in final analysis, on the presence of *conflict*. If you have only a one-way feeling about something—getting out of a burning building, for example, there is not much equivocation about your actions—you get out as soon as possible. This is an escape or avoidance response and, unless it is inhibited or thwarted, you will in this instance experience no conflict and no anxiety. Fear is present in such a case; and fear provokes a one-way-street kind of reaction. If, also, you are invited to a sumptuous meal when you are duly hungry, there is not any approach hesitancy—you go with relish and full appreciation of the repast. There is no conflict here.

Fear and also strong motivation toward a pleasurable goal are, in their separate ways, examples of one-way streets of single purpose motivation. They do not harbor conflict. BUT anxiety does harbor conflict—there we find the ever-present two-way feeling; the mixed up, on-again-off-again, going-both-ways-at-once feeling; a desire to do something pitted against a reluctance, doubt, or failure of confidence. Due to this conflict, anxiety then binds, delays, inhibits you; it makes for confusion and reduces your personal effectiveness and happiness; it causes loss of confidence in yourself as an individual and in your ability to cope with your social and interpersonal environment.

In everything said in this book, speculated about here, or offered as a technique, the coping with anxiety has been the major thrust. You are asked to understand anxiety as a natural kind of reaction to many stressful situations, as a condition that may easily get out of hand, as a condition that all people experience and try to cope with as well as they can, and as a condition that can and does submit to a variety of measures and techniques.

You are asked to see that anxiety can range all the way from mild but annoying instances out to grossly self-defeating cases. You are given a number of "for instances" from individuals' psychotherapy where the underlying conflict and the resultant anxiety are brought under control. And you are given a number of small and useful ways to cope with small and irritating problems related to anxiety.

The coverage of anxiety here—while not guaranteed to span every situation you may encounter—is nonetheless broad and is bound to be effective in many different ways for most people. The test comes in putting the ideas into a working relationship between you and your environment and consistently pushing for the best possible results.

WHEN ALL'S said and done, which chapters were of most value to you? Which ones of least value? Can you learn more for yourself—your own comfort and confidence—by rechecking them?

Index